HOW-TO
EARN MORE USING THE
PROFESSIONAL
EXCELLENCE
SYSTEM
FOR MANAGING
PROFESSIONALS

Peter H. Burgher

The Agnes Press
Unusual Business Books
Utica, Michigan
1985

HOW-TO
EARN MORE USING THE
PROFESSIONAL
EXCELLENCE
SYSTEM
FOR MANAGING
PROFESSIONALS

Library of Congress Cataloguing in Publication Data
Burgher, Peter H.
PROFESSIONAL EXCELLENCE
85-07296

ISBN No. 0-936033-00-2

Produced by The Agnes Press, Unusual Business Books. Printed
by R. R. Donnelley & Sons Company at Crafordsville, Indiana.
Typesetting in Century Schoolbook by Macomb Printing Specialties, Inc. Design of book and jacket by Irene Friedman and Harold
Fryer.

HOW TO EARN MORE USING THE

PROFESSIONAL EXCELLENCE
SYSTEM
FOR MANAGING PROFESSIONALS

TABLE OF CONTENTS

TABLE OF CONTENTS

EXHIBITS (continued)

APPENDICES

Author's preface

For some twenty-four years I have enjoyed the dual role of helping clients manage their businesses while at the same time learning to manage my own. As a managing partner of a big-8 CPA firm, I started in a totally unstructured environment, opening my own new office. That first key assignment was essentially learning by doing, but I had the opportunity to learn from some masters. When the opportunity presented itself I asked such clients as Royal Little, Harvey Sarles, John Keenan, and others who had experienced the responsibility for turning around or redirecting businesses how they plied their trade. Gradually, some theories evolved in my application of what they taught me that I tried first in redirecting organizations of professional people such as a Chamber of Commerce, a Red Cross Chapter, a governmental unit. Then the opportunity came to rebuild a major office of my firm. More evolution and experimentation and learning from others took place. The application was critical and I experimented with teachings from some management development courses developed by a brilliant synthesizer, Ted Sable. More opportunities presented themselves in helping other large professional firms, as their CPA, confessor and consultant. Still more applications became available in other volunteer leadership roles. After ten to twelve years of managing my practice, my theories had become firmed and organized. They were written down and had been applied in numerous cases. They worked.

A first step to this book occurred, however, when my research for an anthology on managing change was going on. "Changement — understanding and managing business change"* is a companion volume to this

---

* Available from Lexington Books, Lexington, Mass., 02175, or by mail order from The Agnes Press.

i

book which weaves my basic theories using the best works written by others that I could find. It has taken retirement from my firm and time for some applied art to finish the work.

Now the task is completed and the PROFES-SIONAL EXCELLENCE approach to managing professionals of all kinds is brought together for your use as well as mine. The book is deliberately brief, you don't need a lot of words to support basic "how to" management tools. If you use them you will find the tools really work and you will have the ability to know how to pull your people to greatness. With them you will earn more than you could before and do it more enjoyably than you would have any other way. Managing professionals can be fun.

Without the help of literally hundreds of people this book would not have been written. Some of them are named above. Others are mentioned in the book. Most important of all is my father, a true professional who taught me to "charge enough so that it hurts" and to respect the people values in life. My thanks to D. C. Graves, editorial critic par excellence, for patient and thorough guidance. Without the editorial guidance of Elinor, my wife, editor and critic, the book would probably not have been slimmed down to the hard hitting and direct management tool it is intended to be.

PHB
August 15, 1985

About the author —

Peter H. Burgher is active in several business fields. He is a director of a company holding certain types of manufacturing businesses, Chairman of the Board of Directors of a technology transfer company and Chairman and President of MARELCO Power Systems, Inc., a high technology manufacturer of electrical equipment. He teaches and consults to professional and industrial concerns on management, turn-arounds, taxation, mergers and acquisitions and troubled-debt situations. For twenty-four years he was with Arthur Young & Company, the last fourteen of which were as managing partner of several offices. His book "Change-ment — understanding and managing business change" was published in 1979 by Lexington Books, D.C. Heath Company. In addition to his business and professional activities, Mr. Burgher serves in leadership roles in the Red Cross, other service organizations and the Center for Science and Technology, in Detroit.

LAYING
THE
FOUNDATION

CHAPTER 1

Introduction
WHAT IS THE PROFESSIONAL EXCELLENCE SYSTEM?

"I have seen the future and it scares the hell out of me." Richard Reeves, reporter, Time Magazine, November 10, 1975.

That statement is typical of the response, these days, of many people. But, it especially characterizes the response of the manager of today's professional organization. Many leaders of professional firms are bothered by the increasing intensity of their businesses, the needs to cope with new conditions (such as advertising) and the increasing competition that pressures from society, Congress and the FTC have pushed upon almost all of the professions today. When you utilize the systematic management methods employed in PROFESSIONAL EXCELLENCE you will be utilizing effective methods to deal with these pressures.

Some professional people really enjoy managing their organizations: but, many professional firm managers do not enjoy the process of management. Some tend to shy away from the necessary but uncomfortable decisions that are commonly associated with the administrative tasks they face. With PROFESSIONAL EXCELLENCE these tasks become easier and the concerns are reduced because management becomes an integrated way of living in the professional environment.

Even though there are unprecedented numbers of people to recruit from, the problems of selecting, motivating and retaining professional people are worse than they ever have been. With PROFESSIONAL EXCELLENCE these problems and concerns become manageable because the tasks of recruiting, managing and developing people are integrated into a cohesive system.

Since the principal costs in any professional organization consist of salary and related indirect costs, the pressures of cost versus revenue have been magnified because salaries carry more of the impact of today's inflationary economy than professional fees. With PROFESSIONAL EXCELLENCE these problems can be managed effectively and earning power maintained and increased.

There is a cohesive system and theory upon which the management of professionals can be based. This system differs in many ways from the approaches typically used for manufacturing or non-service businesses. In over twenty years of managing professional people, I have had the opportunity to develop this system and the theory underlying it. I have had the opportunity of seeing its application in a number of complex and interesting situations, including start-ups and including turn-arounds. The PROFESSIONAL EXCELLENCE system is based upon both my experience and the combined experience of many others, in managing and turning around professional service businesses.

PROFESSIONAL EXCELLENCE is based upon building an organization that will enable you to carry out the destiny of your professional organization as you and your colleagues decide it should be, using two major thrusts:

1. An organization structure that is designed to self-enhance your business objectives, and

2. Management systems that are designed to help your people achieve their chosen individual destinies in harmony, and in furtherance, of the goals of the firm.

The term PROFESSIONAL EXCELLENCE is based upon the POWER TO KNOW AND LEAD IN THE DIRECTIONS YOU WISH. And, it is based on the use of standardized management systems to PULL YOUR ORGANIZATION in those directions. We all know that a mule is a highly intelligent and independent minded creature. Now, it may seem unflattering to compare the people in your organization to the legendary mule, but if you think about it you will recall there is no way you can kick or push your mule to go down a particular path unless he wants to go that way of his own volition. On the other hand, if you take your mule by the halter and lead him in the direction you wish to go, he, sensing that is the direction he wants to go, will proceed willingly. Unflattering as it may seem, your people are much the same as our friend the mule. No amount of kicking and screaming, pushing and cajoling will make them go in directions they do not want to. But, by enhancing their ability to achieve their own objectives, you can PULL them in the direction best for the organization as a whole.

Simply stated, PROFESSIONAL EXCELLENCE is just that, obtaining real professional achievement through the excellence that can be achieved by pulling your people to greatness, to be professionally excellent in every way you want them to be.

There are certain principles upon which PROFES-SIONAL EXCELLENCE is based. These will be developed in the foundation section of the book. With a thorough understanding of these principles and the reasons why the PROFESSIONAL EXCELLENCE system uses the techniques that it requires, the book then moves into a step-by-step description of the system. At the close of each system chapter there is a "how to" list for you to follow and use as a reminder in your day-to-day application of the system.

The system, itself, is not complex. One of its strongest features is the total integration of one element of the system with each other. This enables operating efficiencies and straight forward direction of your professional business to be achieved at the least cost. This is how increased earnings result. With PROFESSIONAL EXCELLENCE you recruit only the people you need. With PROFESSIONAL EXCELLENCE these people are relatively efficient and because they are well motivated and operating harmoniously, they produce a higher level of quality of output than they would if left unstructured and without the system.

In my experience while developing PROFES-SIONAL EXCELLENCE over the years, the offices of my firm that I was responsible for consistently had higher earnings and a higher percentage of return on revenue than most other offices of the firm. Why was this? It was because PROFESSIONAL EXCELLENCE works. By simply and effectively working within a plan, and finding ways to utilize the highest quality personnel producing the highest quality output, my offices were relatively more efficient than others. There is one additional ingredient, however, and that is growth. PROFESSIONAL EXCELLENCE enables you to achieve consistent and dependable growth patterns in directions that you want. I learned early on in my business career that new business development was not simply the task of the managing partner or one or two designated "sales" partners. PROFESSIONAL EXCELLENCE enables you to make business development and growth the function of the entire organization. Obviously, a hundred and fifty or more people can, for example, be much more effective in developing contacts and opportunities than one or two people. PROFESSIONAL EXCELLENCE shows you how to achieve this end.

You earn more money because PROFESSIONAL EXCELLENCE enables your firm to be more efficient. By having your resources in place to meet the growth produced by your plan, your goals for the firm are achieved efficiently and directly. PROFESSIONAL EXCELLENCE works. Try it and I am sure you will find it will work well for you.

CHAPTER 2

PROFESSIONAL PEOPLE ARE DIFFERENT

In its early years, the management consulting firm enjoyed spectacular growth and its four partners and 12 people handled the detail of scheduling, billings, support services, and other administrative tasks in regular democratic meetings. Because of their success the firm grew steadily. The two senior partners decided they needed an experienced operations manager to help them in work assignments and to supervise its execution. After some thought, they did an outside search for an experienced person. Ultimately, they found someone from a client organization who was hired and inserted into the firm as vice-president operations. He seemed ideal for the job even though he came from a different background than most of the consultants in the firm. He was not a theoretician. He had plenty of skills in writing and planning and, for a while, it appeared that a good decision had been made. After six months went by, however, passive resistance to his functioning increased steadily. Since the vice-president was not an authoritarian in style he soon was reduced to sitting at his desk preparing memorandums. The effectiveness of the staff began to drop, morale hit bottom and finally the vice-president was discharged after a painful series of episodes where the partners were unable to back his decisions regarding work assignments and quality controls.

Why did this happen? The obvious answer is that they made a bad choice. It is not as simple as that. We all know the situation where the large law firm hires an internal administrator whose authority is perceived by the lawyers in the firm as negligible because "he is not a lawyer." That fact is closer to the truth than the conclusion in our example above that the man was simply a poor choice. Professional people believe that they are different and they are often unwilling to accept the leadership of people who are different from them.

In fact, professional people are not totally different from other people in our business world. The differences that do exist, however, are important. When you discuss with an accountant, lawyer, architect, consultant or physician the nature of his business, very often you will find that he sincerely believes his "business" is not a business. The typical professional will dispute the idea that he is in business per se. The personal characteristics that tend to cause certain individuals to seek a professional service livelihood mitigate against such persons being interested in the financial and managerial aspects of their occupations. There are, of course, some outstanding exceptions.

For example, despite notable exceptions, many people that seek the professions often profess they do not like to sell. "Selling cheapens the profession" is one way this is expressed. (Unfortunately, selling has become a way of life and is an economic necessity for any profession — it is how you sell, as we will see later, that makes the difference.) What the professional is most likely referring to when he denegrates selling is, on close inspection, the outgoing, agressive (and risky) activities commonly associated with selling industrial or consumer goods. The fact that such associations are

7

not founded on fact does little to change professionals' perceptions. And even though such assumptions about selling are not applicable to professional work, they are widely held.

What the professional really means, is that he seeks to avoid what he perceives the risk of failure! The same applies to other aspects of professional life such as the avoidance of billing clients that many professionals display . . . seeking to avoid possible rejection, dispute or the appearance of failure. In consulting with professional firms and in talks with professional groups, I have characterized this feeling as "the essential feeling of being unworthy." In other words, the professional person has a personality characteristic that does not require the constant ego reward of your typical huckster. His personality is more likely a reflective one. And, being reflective, the profesional knows that he is not capable of doing everything. Being intelligent he thinks his needs over and recognizes that there are some things that can go wrong. Of course, the perception of things going wrong is usually higher in areas of unfamiliarity. Until recently, professionals simply did not have to sell the way other people do and thus the entire area of selling is an unfamiliar one. Because of these social and personal characteristics, the professional feels that he is unable to do what he is not used to doing. Thus, he feels "unworthy".

A useful way of looking at the personality types that make up most professionals is through the personality or style indicator systems that have been developed for testing purposes. One is the Myers-Briggs Indicator System, the characteristics of which are shown in Exhibit 1. Study these definitions for a moment and see how you fit in your own opinion among the eight choices given. Usually a four characteristic definition is used for each individual (like E N T J). Myers-Briggs is one of the best of many such systems

8

and is available through Consultant Psychologists Press, Inc.* Whether extraverted or introverted, professionals have generally common personality characteristics. By far the strongest characteristics are those of thinking and judging, as opposed to feeling and perception. Look at Exhibit 2 which displays the actual characteristics of a group of professionals tested in 1979 for their personality types using the Myers-Briggs System. The strongest characteristic is the one underlined. Notice that fully a third have as their strongest characteristics that of "thinking." Many professionals will also be very strong in "judging" attitude, that is they like a planned, decided and orderly way of life better than a flexible and spontaneous one. You might consider having someone test your personnel and yourself using a system like Myers-Briggs because it will help you determine the characteristics of the leadership group that will best lead those in your organization.

---

* 577 College Ave., Palo Alto, CA 94306 — Information reproduced with permission.

EXHIBIT 1.
MYERS-BRIGGS TYPE INDICATOR

E An E for extraversion probably means you relate more easily to the outer world of people and things than to the inner world of ideas.

I An I for introversion probably means you relate more easily to the inner world of ideas than to the outer world of people and things.

S An S for sensing probably means you would rather work with known facts than look for possibilities and relationships.

N An N for intuition probably means you would rather look for possibilities and relationships than work with known facts.

T A T for thinking probably means you base your judgments more on impersonal analysis and logic than on personal values.

F An F for feeling probably means you base your judgments more on personal values than on impersonal analysis and logic.

J A J for the judging attitude probably means you like a planned, decided, orderly way of life better than a flexible, spontaneous way.

P A P for the perceptive attitude probably means you like a flexible spontaneous way of life better than a planned, decided, orderly way.

EXHIBIT 2
A TYPICAL CONSULTING GROUP

Extraverted Types	Introverted Types
E S <u>T</u> J — 2	I S <u>T</u> P — 1
E N <u>T</u> J— 10	I N <u>T</u> P — 7
E S <u>F</u> J —	I S <u>F</u> P — 1
E N <u>F</u> J — 4	I N <u>F</u> P — 3
E <u>S</u> T P — 3	I <u>S</u> T J — 9
E <u>S</u> F P —	I <u>S</u> F J —
E <u>N</u> T P — 6	I <u>N</u> T J — 9
E <u>N</u> F P — <u>4</u>	I <u>N</u> F J — <u>3</u>
Total 29	Total 33

Myers-Briggs Profiles

There are no right and wrong attitudes or personality characteristics but a realistic understanding of the personality characteristics of the professional, and especially your people, will help you better understand how to lead them. Thinking types of people, for example, do not like to sell. Feeling types of people need thinkers around to help them analyze and organize their work. Intuitive people bring up new possibilities, supply ingenuity, sense coming changes and have boundless enthusiasm. If your people share these characteristics, it is easy to understand why they will sometimes seem to be grumpy, lack enthusiasm, find all the flaws and none of the possibilities and dislike advertising and selling to the nth degree. While you are thinking about the people in your organization look at the high points of personality on Exhibit 1 for the typical professional. He will be an E N T J or an I N T J, typically. Such people cannot be bullied and need real leadership in order to perform at their very best.

With PROFESSIONAL EXCELLENCE, you will be in position to help them achieve their highest levels of potential. As we will see in Chapter 7 and Chapter 9, PROFESSIONAL EXCELLENCE relies on enabling the individual to seek his highest level of achievement by his own means, leading him to his best rather than by pushing.

Professionals are different and the things that are needed to motivate are more different still. Next, we will define the professional.

CHAPTER 3

WHAT IS
A PROFESSIONAL?

The PROFESSIONAL EXCELLENCE system is not for everyone. It only works with people who are what we will be referring to as "professionals" throughout the book.

You can look at professionals in basically two ways. First you can look at the things they do for a living.

The term professional includes the following occupations: doctor, lawyer, accountant, architect, engineer, nurse, teacher, researcher, social worker, professor, clergyman, artist, writer, actor, actuary, auditor, investment advisor, fund raiser, advertising executive, copywriter, editor, newswriter, museum curator, sheriff, investigator, law officer, and many more activities which can truly be described as professional in nature.

This brings us to the second definition of professional. You will note that a single strong characteristic of the above occupations is the lack of dealing with tangible goods or commodities. It is possible to be professional and deal with commodities, such as a stockbroker would, but the salient characteristic of a professional is that he deals with intangibles and abstract ideas as opposed to the physical manipulation of goods or the environment. Professionals tend to operate in what appear to be democratic (more about this later) horizontally decentralized organizations. They tend to like extensive autonomy and seem happiest when they are free of need to coordinate closely with their peers. Good professionals are generally responsible, highly motivated and dedicated to the work and the people they serve. They tend to value highly the relationship they have with their clients. A key characteristic of professionals is that, because their professionalism is attributable to their expertise and management of the abstract (an idealogical specialty of their profession) their loyalty tends to be to the profession and not to the organization in which they serve.

The management of professionals can be applied with considerable success to all of the people listed in the above occupations. I have found, for example, that many of the techniques described in this book were applicable when I was Chairman of the Board of the third largest Red Cross Chapter in the nation. There, we had five hundred staff people and some thirty-three thousand volunteers integrated into a largely harmonious organization having multiple goals and many services. Giving these people the opportunity to set and work toward their own goals was my greatest contribution to this organization. Through PROFESSIONAL EXCELLENCE I was able to show them how their needs could coincide with those of the organization and, as a consequence, they developed their own strong sense of direction and moved in a businesslike way toward the goals of the organization.

As a professional, you are special too. Recognizing your own strengths and weaknesses will help you enhance the strengths and overcome the weaknesses of the people with whom you work. Since professional people are different from one and another it is useful to know the areas in which these differences occur. The differences become important when we consider how to motivate professionals as we do in the next chapter.

CHAPTER 4

MOTIVATING THE PROFESSIONAL PERSON

"Take a look at yourself and you can look at others differently," goes an anonymous saying that has considerable weight to it. In conducting management development courses and through many discussions with boards and management committees of client firms, I have found a useful technique is to ask them what are the conditions they feel motivate and demotivate them as individuals. You are a professional manager; consider the things that "turn you on" and the conditions that "turn you off." In my experience the responses to these questions tend to be typical regardless of the respondents' particular calling. Be they accountants, engineers, lawyers or actuaries their responses have similar characteristics.

Exhibit 3 shows the responses of a particular seminar in which I listed on a chalk board the "turn ons" and "turn offs" the people in that seminar thought most affected their attitude toward their work. First, I segregated the people according to their level of seniority and experience and appointed a leader to act as a spokesman for each group. The leaders then gathered the views of their groups' members and posted them for all in the seminar to see. Two things stand out.

EXHIBIT 3
Sample lists of profesional "turn-ons" and "turn-offs"

STAFF

On
- Recognition
- Self-satisfaction
- Challenge
- Association
- Compensation
- Contribution
- Self-development
- Personal interest

Off
- Lack of respect
- Autocratic aura
- Blocking
- No feedback
- No structure

MIDDLE SUPERVISORS

On
- Recognition
- Creative opportunity
- Respect
- Cooperation
- Common values
- Professional growth
- Stimulated environment

Off
- Blocking
- No respect
- Stymied creativity
- Putting in time
- Wastes
- Incompetence

SENIOR SUPERVISORS

On
- Development
- Challenge
- Freedom
- Recognition
- Self-selectivity

Off
- Poor interrelationships
- No recognition
- No reliance
- Poor communication
- No teamwork
- Long hours
- Personal sacrifice
- No opportunity

On
- Good work
- Professional atmosphere
- Responsibility
- Good feedback
- Team and identity

Off
- Uninteresting work
- No recognition
- Overtime, travel
- Family pressures
- Unjust blame
- Poor communication
- No consultation
- Conflicts

First there are many similarities between the groups regardless of level. Second, there was a migration in emphasis from the lowest group to the highest group. Housekeeping items tended to have apparently more importance the higher an individual moved in that particular organization. Look closely at Exhibit 3 to identify the similarities and trends. Don't be mislead by this migration.

The reason that what appear to be housekeeping items (such as overtime and excessive travel) loom in higher importance in the higher level group is due to the fact that the individuals' inherent work satisfaction is probably better defined and has become stronger as they move up in the organization. Note that the housekeeping items only provide "turn-offs" . . . that is, the presence of a negative housekeeping item is a "turn-off." There is no indicated need, in this group, for positive housekeeping items as "turn-ons."

It is important to recognize the characteristics of the kind of things that motivate and demotivate professional people. That is why I have asked you to list for yourself, if you can do it objectively, the factors that you consider most important in your life. If you can do it objectively the chances are you will find your factors are very similar to those of the typical group in Exhibit 3.

In my experience, there are certain factors that are named more than others even though there are many additional factors that could conceivably be named depending upon the participants' levels or other variations in group makeup. To summarize, the strongest profesional "turn-on" are:

TURN-ONS
— *The opportunity to excel*

— *An atmosphere of self development*

— *Supportive personal relationships*

— Adequate recognition of the individual's contribution

— Constructive, creative work

— Superiors interested in the individual's role in the organization

— Professional independence

Some of the less frequently cited factors include: association with knowledgable people, opportunities to be creative and flexible, freedom to develop one's own style, recognition for being on a valued team, and the ability to help others grow. Notice the continuing absence of traditional housekeeping values and the strong bias toward individual rather than group recognition. Personal needs of these types tend to predict the kinds of persons capable of better client service than individuals who do not know "who" they are and do not care what they are doing.

Now let us consider the factors that tend to reduce professionals' performance and the desire to perform well. When I was moved into a classic turnaround situation some years ago as a managing partner of one of the largest offices of my firm, I found a complex mix of undercurrents that indicated that something was clearly wrong with the attitudes of the personnel in the organization. The office had not been performing well for some years. One partner, a senior and very well liked person, had been placed in charge of personnel. He was a man who could not say "no" to anybody. I later determined that the inability to say "no" was, at once, both the reason he was so well liked personally and a strong contributor to the weakness of the organization. As I started routine structured interviews with the staff people in the office, I learned that a major concern existed about a phenomenon they called "blockage." They perceived that people at certain levels had

18

risen as far as they could go and were going to stay there the rest of their working lives, thus "blocking" the progress of persons lower down in the organization. Even though a fairly good job had been done in hiring new recruits, these new young and agressive people believed they had no place to go due to the blockage from their peers immediately above them. How did the blockage occur? It arose because the senior personnel partner simply could not tell some of the managers in the organization that they were better off moving out to industry or to new types of jobs where their growth could continue. Because he could not say "no", he could not tell anyone their career was limited. He was widely viewed as being ineffectual and the "blockage" theory was very strong. It took several years to overcome this syndrome and it required great care to ease out those whose positions blocked the development of others.

Following is a listing of the motivation reducing factors most often listed by professionals in work sessions such as I have described above:

TURN-OFFS
— *Blocked personal growth*
— *Little or no feedback*
— *Unstructured organization*
— *Lack of respect for work product*
— *Ineffectual leaders and peers*
— *Inadequate compensation*
— *Firm not coping with its problems*
— *Not being consulted*

These factors are similar for accountants <u>and</u> for salesmen! While they are often important to people in manufacturing organization, they are of far more importance to people working in professional capacities and dealing with abstractions. Where work product is

19

intangible, the existence of the above "turn-offs" are much more important than where the work product can be measured in specific units or output or "machines shipped."

Less cited but mentioned often enough for comment as professional "turn-offs" are autocratic styles of leadership, unclear or unreasonable constraints, wasted time or efforts, inability to be creative, excessive time requirements, pettiness or politics.

The choice of politics as a "turn-off" should be regarded with skepticism since it generally appears that people who prefer working in a professional environment are capable of politics and petty jealousies at the highest level. When politics are perceived to be an acceptable method of coping with otherwise unsatisfactory conditions, professional people can perform extremely well. Whether they exercise their abilities may depend upon the history and need of related patterns.

Generally, persons in professional firm management find it easy to agree that their people will be motivated or demotivated by conditions similar to those described above and in Exhibit 3. The "crunch in managing professionals" comes in developing and applying management techniques that will overcome problems of 1) the absence of "turn-ons" or 2) the presence of "turn-offs" in your professional organization. That is what managing professional service firms and professional people is all about. The PROFESSIONAL EXCELLENCE system depends upon using an integrated approach to creating environmental factors and personal conditions that will reinforce the positive and tend to eliminate the negative factors in the "turn-ons" and "turn-offs" that make you and your people tick.

First, let us take a studied look at the structure of the professional firm so we will have a basis for meeting the organizational as well as the personal needs of the professional person.

CHAPTER 5

THE STRUCTURE OF THE PROFESSIONAL FIRM

Recently, a group of psychologists representing the senior management of a firm of 43 professionals came to me with a serious crisis. Given the nature of professionals, they pointed out, none of them wanted an immediate superior between him and the Chief Executive Officer. In this case, all 43 psychologists had been taking their questions, complaints, problems, and management ideas to one Chief Executive Officer. He, in turn, was trying to deal with all of them, individually, plus providing important consulting services to the firms two major clients. The Chief Executive was a brilliant, introverted and energetic person. His pride said to him that he could come up with a great solution to almost every problem his people brought to him. Indeed, until his heart attack, he boasted about his "open door" policies and his ability to deal with everything that came his way. With his introverted personality, however, this high quality of people contact was very stressful to him and evidently led to the physical problems that precipitated his attack. When the organization reached a crisis of his making, no one had been prepared to succeed him in the Chief Executive job.

Some broad policies with clear guidelines to the

professionals in the organization might have saved the Chief Executive's life.

In an interesting article in the Financial Analysts Journal, James Balog points out that few investment analyists begin their careers thinking they will be analyists forever; most regard the position as a stepping stone to something else. But while career progress in the investment industry consists of moving toward the top, there are only a few jobs at the top of the investment research business. With no clearcut pathway to those jobs, analyists at mid-career begin to wonder whether they can keep the creative juices flowing for the rest of their working lives. This creates mid-life crisis and promotes high turnover in the ranks of the analyist group. Look at Exhibit 4 for a graphic depiction of the power pyramid in an industrial concern as opposed to that commonly associated with the investment research business.

"If you want someone to build you a satellite to orbit sixty thousand miles around the earth to detect nuclear earth explosions in millions of miles of space, you have got to have an organization that is capable of coming up with highly creative thinking," says an executive of TRW, Inc. The kind of advanced products and service that TRW's systems group provides requires that they have imaginative minds and an atmosphere that is open and encourages people to use their minds without many of the constraints of traditional organizations.

So, what did TRW do? They analyzed the nature of their professional service delivery system and reorganized it to what they termed a "matrix" system of management in which projects were broken into individual modules that were assigned to specific groups or teams. Then, team building exercises and courses were employed to facilitate the adaptation of traditional minded managers to the new group management

EXHIBIT 4

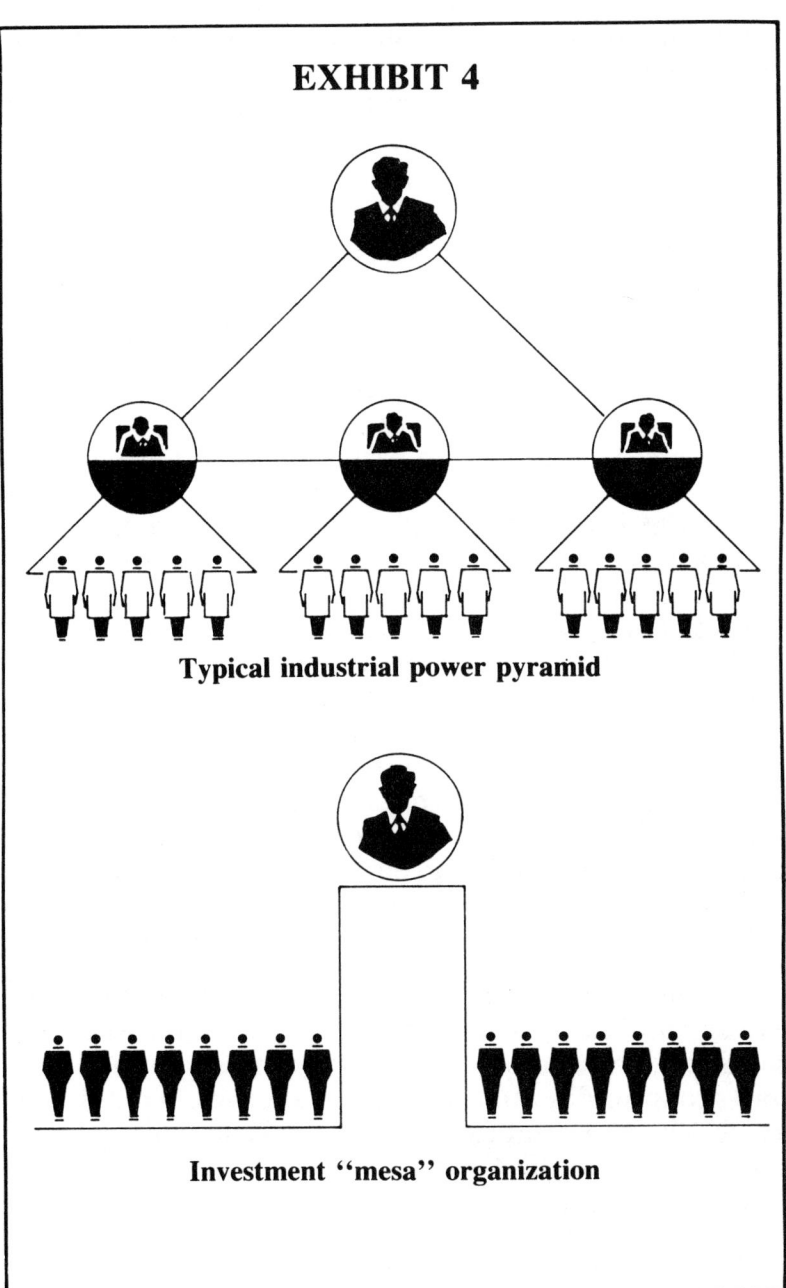

Typical industrial power pyramid

Investment "mesa" organization

approach. More than a third of TRW's over sixteen thousand employees are engineers or scientists. A properly structured management approach was the only way to motivate and utilize these people effectively.

There are a number of theories about the ways in which managers behave. One theory holds that there is a progression from "doing" to "managing" as responsibility increases, as shown in Exhibit 5. There is much less movement from "doing" to "managing" between the bottom and the top of the professional firm, and TRW's response to its managerial needs for engineers and scientists gave recognition to this fact in setting the optimal organization size of a small productive group. The exact equation of the difference between movement from doing to managing between manufacturing versus professional firms is unimportant. It may be a function of one half or less in the professional firm than that of a product creating industrial organization.

Many professionals view their organizations much like the mesa pictured in Exhibit 4. In fact, this is not entirely true either. The best description of the optimal professional organization has been made by a University of Michigan Professor, Dr. Rensis Likert. In his writings on the linking-pin concept, Likert sets forth a theory of overlapping groups in organizations. Basically the "linking-pin" in his theory is the person who belongs to two groups within the organization.

These groups can be ad hoc or permanent. They can be administrative or functional. Usually, according to Likert, the "linking-pin" individual is a superior in one group and a subordinate in another. This a very much like the condition in the professional organization. Look at Exhibit 6 for a pictorial representation of Likert's "linking-pin" theory.

This definition of the "linking-pin" may appear merely to be a restatement of the functions of any man-

EXHIBIT 5

Typical view of the progression from worker to manager

MOSTLY SUPERVISING

Supervising groups	TOP MANAGEMENT
Supervising limited numbers	MIDDLE MANAGEMENT
One on one supervision	LINE MANAGEMENT
Doing	WORK FORCE

MOSTLY DOING

ager in any unit in any unit in an organization. The principal difference in the "linking-pin" concept lies in the manager's perception of his job and his behavior growing out of this perception. In the group theory of organization, the manager becomes a "linking-pin" in that he not only serves as a connector of two groups but he is actually a member of two groups:

1. He is a member of a group of his peers, all heads of departments, who may constitute a group roughly called middle management in some organizations, reporting to a Chief Executive Officer and,

2. He also belongs to the group or team that he heads, and he views himself not as a commander or director but as a member of that team.

In this context, Likert stresses the crucial importance of the manager's interaction with his group. Likert advocates open communication within the group, development of a mutual trust, consensus decision making, group goal setting, definition of roles and shared responsibility. These result in group accountability, group loyalty, cohesiveness, and better identification of the individual with the groups goals. Obviously, these conditions are partially dependent on the degree of interaction the manager has with his group and the degree of influence it exerts.

EXHIBIT 6
Likert's "linking-pin" organization

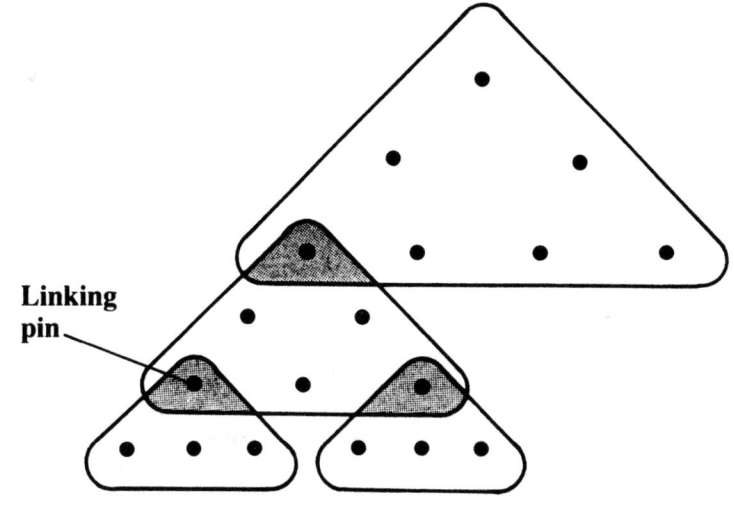

Linking pin

  Organization overlap

In the professional firm there is not much movement from "doing" to "managing" as noted above, between the bottom and top of the firm. Each level has its own limited span of command. Power depends not on what one does as much as it depends upon how broad one's pyramid is, often a function of how many people one supervises. Look at Exhibit 7 for a graphic display of the typical professional's pyramids. In the professional pyramid there is some overlap at all levels but it is greatest at the staff professional level where members of one team may also simultaneously be assigned to other teams on which they work from time to time. Managers and supervisors may be responsible for one or more teams depending on their circumstances, engagement assignments, and the complexity of the underlying work.

In professional firms, income, perquisites and rank tend to follow the size of the pyramid base. Thus, personal development will tend to follow the individual's ability to expand the number of people he supervises. It also relates to the number of jobs and complexity of the jobs he controls, the new clients he obtains and similar factors.

Obviously, the professional pyramid will vary in size and shape depending upon the particular professional discipline involved. In public accounting firms, the pyramid can get very large and the numbers of individuals rather sizeable. In the case of physicians, on the other hand, even in the largest clinics, the pyramids are not very broad at the bottom. The differences relate largely to the amount of personal contact between the professionals and other activities unrelated to the technological work being done.

EXHIBIT 7
The professional pyramid

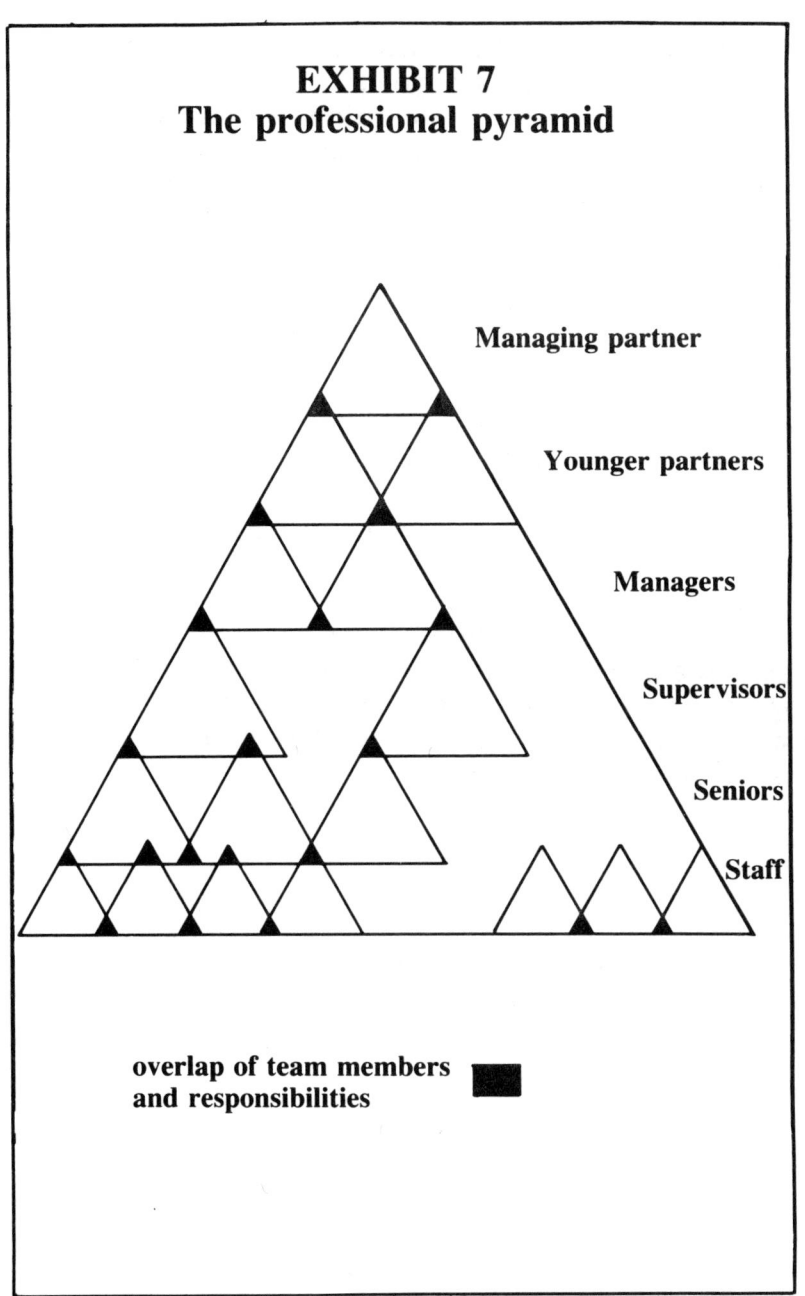

Managing partner

Younger partners

Managers

Supervisors

Seniors

Staff

overlap of team members
and responsibilities

In PROFESSIONAL EXCELLENCE, motivating professionals involves developing in them an understanding of these facts concerning the nature of professional organizations. By setting their goals, for personal growth, salary, and other factors, they commit themselves to advancement in the organization in terms of the size and complexity of the pyramid they manage. Demonstrating these relationships is a integral part of the PROFESSIONAL EXCELLENCE process. In discussing career opportunities with the individual professional, it is easy to demonstrate that technical knowledge alone (while a given for advancement) is not the sole criterion for personal growth. Growth potential can be infinite since it depends upon the size of the individual's pyramid. In PROFESSIONAL EXCELLENCE you make this understanding an ordinary part of the day-to-day process so that it becomes automatic for the individual professional. Next, we shall examine a conceptual view of professionalism so that we start applying PROFESSIONAL EXCELLENCE with an agreed and common understanding of what it is we are trying to manage.

CHAPTER **6**

A CONCEPTUAL VIEW OF PROFESSIONALISM

In recent years there have been tremendous changes in the CPA profession, the effects of which have not been clearly understood by most of those involved. Social and personal changes of the highest magnitude have taken place where the CPA firms were totally unprepared for them. The profession had no knowledge at the beginning of this process of the effects they were about to create. Similar changes have occurred in other professions, but few are as dramatic and complex as the CPA's situation. The story is an interesting one. Starting from the Bar-Chris case in the 60's and the high flying stocks and merger movement of the late 60's and early 70's, the attention of Congress and the public was focused on the CPA profession in a most unsatisfactory way. CPA's were blamed for management excesses and failures such as Penn Central, Equity Funding and others. Under pressure from Congress and the SEC, the American Institute of CPA's promulgated a rule requiring mandatory rotation of client serving partners who handled publicly held companies. The theory, under these new rules, was that independence would be assured through mandatory rotation. Naively, the profession hoped that earlier perceived abuses would thus be ended. Today, a partner can serve his publicly held client no more than five years whereas before the new rule he could serve his client for an indefinite period. Interestingly, however, the profession failed to recognize in agreeing to these rules that the major "possession" of each client handling partner is their clients of long standing. As a consequence, the new rules have created paranoia in the ranks of the partners of major CPA firms. The one thing a partner could rely upon for strength in dealing with his other partners has been removed from him. No longer can he count forevermore on the billings of "his" precious clients.

Some very interesting side effects have arisen from this situation. One of these is the well publicized overturn of several major CPA firms' carefully laid succession plans in recent years. Another effect is the selection of the individuals who have become the new generation of leaders in the CPA firms as the 1950's generation came to retirement. The new generation of leaders has been largely selected from the ranks of the good technicians rather than persons selected for their managerial competence. The selections were made using the "he's just like us" syndrome, under the assumption that by appointing a good technician to the senior job the very upset and disturbed rank and file partners will feel comfortable that they are dealing with one of their own kind. This syndrome will probably pay off in the next five years with some management disasters, widely varying performance in a number of firms and declining profitability. In fact, declining profitability is already apparent in some firms as the marketplace has forced severe price cutting in reaction to the perceived similarity of CPA firms audit services.

The pyramid is difficult for people in most professional groups to recognize. Such organizations tend to be horizontally decentraliized and tend to exhibit considerable autonomy among their members. This personal autonomy causes professionals to believe their organizations are functioning in a democratic manner. You and I know this is patently not true but try to explain that to some of your younger partners who feel they have finally "arrived" and have the right to express their views and take action on almost anything that comes into their heads. For most professional groups, and especially those with significant size, democracy simply does not exist.

It cannot be! Larger professional organizations require such extensive coordination of activities and so many overlapping and mutually dependent services that they cannot be managed on an unplanned basis. In PROFESSIONAL EXCELLENCE, we use the professional's need for participation and empathy as a positive force in making the planning and organization palatable. By requiring participation in a positive way, we overcome the resentment the profesional naturally harbors for businesslike approaches to his needs.

Since there is a highly personal relationship between almost any professional and the client or persons that he serves, loyalty is usually stronger to the client than to the professional organization. Look back at the personality characteristics that professionals display, as discussed in Chapter 3, and you will see why many professionals like being insulated from the business pressures of contemporary life. Some say this is because professionals fear exposure to general business decisions and problems. No so! In fact, it is more likely attributable to the professionals' personality characteristics requiring the thinker and judger to be able to expertise as a way of earning his living. Expertising is more meaningful to the thinker and judger than getting things done as a manager. A professional does not have to be an independent contractor to prefer his technological work to managerial work. As a result, his loyalty is, as stated above, to his client and to his "work".

Often, there is a technical similarity (almost to the point of exact duplication) between the work done by a professional firm for one client and that done for another. This similarity also extends to the work done by one professional firm and another. It is easy for a professional to pick up and move from one client to another and from one firm to another. Thus, there can be a high degree of mobility by professional people among firms.

The net result is a loyalty to the profession rather than to the organization. These characteristics both work "against" the firm and are some of the reasons why the "turn-ons" and "turn-offs" are the motivating factors for typical professionals. PROFESSIONAL EXCELLENCE utilizes a technique of demonstrating to the professional that he can achieve his goals only within the organization in which he is located. This helps to overcome the problem of loyalty to the profession.

When professional firms get into managerial difficulty, their managers tend to respond with the same types of actions as do managers in other types of business. Unfortunately, however, the typical managerial response will exacerbate the difficulties of the situation rather than provide improvement. Look at Exhibit 8 for a description of some typical business needs and some typical managerial responses. For background reading on this point, see Dr. Henry Mintzberg's "The Structuring of Organizations" published by Prentice-Hall in 1979.

One typical response to the case of managerial difficulties in a professional firm, just as it might be in any other type of organization is to tighten controls. To some extent, tightening controls may be desirable and necessary in any organization. But, it can reach a threshold of effectiveness more rapidly in a professional firm than in a manufacturing establishment. The types of controls needed in professional firms are far different than those needed in the creation of physical products. For example, in a machining operation a typical control might be a "go-no-go" gauge. It is conceptually impossible to utilize a gauge in evaluating the "correctness" of professional work output. Profesional work has to be evaluated on the same thoughtful basis as it was produced. Professionals may respond to quality control problems by saying, "every report has to be written exactly this way." And professional people will respond to that type of control with resentment and anger because they know no two client situations require exactly the same type of report or response.

In professional firms, bureaucracy tends to work against effectiveness in maintaining the needed creative and aggressive atmosphere that makes for real client service and positive growth patterns. The result of the typical responses given in Exhibit 8 will generally be to reduce service to an impersonal level and thus really discourage those who remain with the organization. This will, obviously, eventually discourage the clients as well. The answer in a professional context is that complex work cannot be effectively performed unless it is under the control of the operator who does it. The key to good quality, for example, is to have good quality people and have them properly trained. No amount of report review or working paper studies will make up for having a sloppy person on the job.

PROFESSIONAL EXCELLENCE depends upon building a structure that will standardize your firm's work approach and standardize your peoples' attitudes toward the firm. PROFESSIONAL EXCELLENCE involves top leadership in a pull to centralize decision making and at the same time promote participation in goal setting at all levels. PROFESSIONAL EXCEL-

EXHIBIT 8
Business needs
and business responses

Typical need	Typical responses
Coordination among line and support staff	**Standardization of** work outputs
Discretion to apply appropriate skills to client need	**Direction** of input from managerial hierarchy
Innovation to meet changing client requirements	**Routinization** of tasks and service application

LENCE permits centralization both vertically and horizontally and allows the professional organization to expand to as broad a pyramid base as is necessary to meet its organizational needs. PROFESSIONAL EXCELLENCE makes it positive for professionals to collaberate within their organization.

The next section of this book is a summary of the PROFESSIONAL EXCELLENCE tools that are derived from the foregoing discussion of professionals, motivating them, structuring the firm and understanding professionalism.

SUMMARY OF PROFESSIONAL EXCELLENCE TOOLS

Since the structure of the professional firm is not the same as other businesses, professional people tend to fall into the trap of forgetting they are in business. PROFESSIONAL EXCELLENCE permits an appropriate recognition of the business attributes of the firm with an environment that encourages personal achievement and development. Recognition of an ideal structure for the firm permits us to develop an approach to the "how-to" and accomplish a motivating atmosphere that will make it all possible. The tools used in PROFESSIONAL EXCELLENCE to develop professional firms to their highest potential are the following:

1. Upward mobility climate
2. Participative management style
3. Continued professional development
4. Uniform definition of responsibilities and levels
5. Understand the roles your people play
6. Regular well-structured performance appraisals
7. Practice development as a regular thing
8. Careful and strategic hiring
9. A rational business plan

In the next sections of this book we will amplify

the means by which PROFESSIONAL EXCELLENCE enables these conditions to be achieved. PROFESSIONAL EXCELLENCE has proved to be an effective management approach because it is based upon the understanding in Chapters 1-6 which gave rise to the conceptual view of the tools that must be used. In its simplest terms, the "how-to" tools utilized in PROFESSIONAL EXCELLENCE involve bringing participants at all levels into the management of the organization in appropriate ways and bootstrapping the organization into effectiveness through providing each professional with what he needs to reach his highest effectiveness.

USING
THE
SYSTEM

CHAPTER 7

CREATE AN UPWARD MOBILITY CLIMATE

A large and fairly prestigious, and outwardly successful, law firm called me for consultation with some of the senior partners not too long ago. Their concern that caused them to call upon me was manifested in one serious symptom. It appeared, by comparisons made with other law firms, that there was excessive turnover among the group of non-partner lawyers whom they called "associates." This firm had some one hundred ten lawyers, all told, including partners and associates. The senior partners were concerned about the turnover symptom. Based upon extended discussion among themselves, the partners had decided to make significant increases in compensation levels. They expected that a massive pay change would reduce turnover. When these increased compensation amounts were pushed into their budget calculations, they became concerned about their ability to handle the salary changes without a significant reduction in partner income.

I cautioned them about taking precipitous action, because my review of their compensation structure indicated it was not out of line with statistics published by the bar association to which they belonged and my experience with professional firms in the general area of their operation. Conversations with a number of partners and associates indicated that the concern about excessive turnover was valid. Causes for the turnover were not clear to the partners, but became readily apparent from my discussions with the associates. The firm had only two levels of recognition. One was either a partner or one was not. Although there were some subtle and occasionally distinct recognition factors, associates were, for the most part, indistinguishable from one and another. About the only differentiating factor one could notice was the fact that some associates seemed to get better cases and work with the more agressive partners, than others.

I recommended the firm adopt a system of recognition levels and pay differentials that permitted promotions to be made within the associate group from time to time. The associates' principal problem was that they could not determine how well they were doing or whether they were succeeding or not. After six to eight years at the associate level with no discernable recognition, the typical associate would become concerned as to whether he was making progress toward his partnership goal. Some associates would make it after eight years and some would not. The frustration of those who were nearing the critical step was apparent. By installing a system of small and recognizable promotions, the partners could signal to each of the associates how they were doing.

Also, the new system would permit those associates who were not measuring up to appraise what needed to be done to achieve the partners' expectations, before it was too late for appropriate changes to be made.

As we discussed in the section concerning the nature of professional people, the maintainence of an up-ward mobility climate is of paramount importance in managing professional people.

Since professionals have a primary need to see that they can achieve continued personal growth and that this growth will result in upward movement within the organization and toward their career goals, the organization must have a way of responding to this need. Several methods are useful.

Consistent use and reference to the organizational diagram and concepts described in the pyramid approach set forth in Chapters 5 and 6, will help reduce the tendency of the individual to believe that his success requires someone else to fail. In fact, the individual's success is dependent upon increasing the size of his pyramid. Use the pyramid concept in management development seminars, meetings, planning sessions and other gatherings where the organization's structure and goals are discussed with the professional group. By doing this, you can illustrate the realities of how an organization can be expanded and how the individual's personal growth is tied to the advancement of his capabilities and the expansion of the organization.

Also you must maintain a balance in numbers at all levels to maintain the pyramid in fact. Disproportion at one or more levels will distort your cost and revenue structure. Importantly, too, it will reduce the effectiveness of individual's advancement based on moving up and broadening the base of the structure (see Appendix 5 for an example of planning a proper pyramid for growth).

In Appendix 1 there is set forth a "career capability profile" which is an example of a useful way to organize small and frequent promotions along lines that are meaningful to the professional person. The career capability profile is just an example of how it might be done in one type of professional firm. You can easily create one for your organization by analyzing the significant changes in duties and scope of control during the evolution of a typical professional person's career in your profession. In reviewing the career capability profile, you will note that both managerial and marketing skills are emphasized. If technical skills can be successfully differentiated in small incremental levels, they should be included in the career capability profile as well.

Once you have developed a viable career capability profile you are then in a position to do what I recommended for the law firm described above. Frequent, small and differentiable promotions within the organization will demonstrate and record mobility. Since there are invariably several levels of skill and responsibility within each broad grouping of titles in a professional organization, giving recognition to changes in status is an easy next step. In the office of my CPA firm that I was responsible for, semi-annual formal grade level changes (i.e. "promotions") converted the facts of life into a demonstration of upward mobility. Not everybody was "promoted" every six months, in fact it took about 1½ to 2 years to achieve one — but, twice a year everyone was reviewed and considered. And, all people in the organization knew that.

Each change should carry with it some recognition in change in status beyond the added responsibilities that are given. One way of converting the need for salary changes from the typical bureaucratic annual inflationary increase to a system based upon changes in responsibility is to couple a "salary model" with the career capability profile. See the typical salary model in Appendix 2. A salary model is a simple grid system that applies qualitative evaluations from poor performance to superior performance to changes in grade level. A salary model with a grid system as shown in Appendix 2 will enable top management, assuming fairness in application, to demonstrate the meaningfulness of the capability profile and the fact that upward mobility will result if performance warrants it.

There is a danger that the appearance of rigidity can result from misapplication of these techniques. One approach, and the best one that I have found, is to involve the entire professional group in determining who should be promoted and why. This has the benefit of creating a sense of participation (described in Chapter 8 which follows) and helps to assure meaningful performance appraisals (described in Chapter 11).

To achieve this involvement, periodically poll each group or level concerning their perceptions of the performance of the individuals immediately below them. For example, if you have a group of managers whose next immediate subordinates are "seniors", the managers would be polled every six months regarding the senior's performance. The managers would be responsible for coming up with a recommended promotion list to be submitted to top management. Since the criteria for promotion to manager are clearly described in the career capability profile for the organization, there should be relatively few mismatches and mistakes. By involving the people whose responsibility it is to develop and promote those immediately below them, the barriers of rigidity can really be reduced. Be careful to document in your files and to explain to your people the promotions that are not made despite group recommendations. The final decision should always belong to top management, but if group recommendations miss some important problem, for example, be sure to let them know why their recommendations are not followed. This is important for E E O (equal employment opportunity) and for morale and motivational considerations.

There is no right or wrong to the number and extent of grade levels. Obviously, your career capability profile and your salary model must track each other exactly. They should both recognize what happens in your profession outside of your firm or business unit. As long as there is a discernable and meaningful difference in responsibility that can be documented, frequent promotions will work to demonstrate an upward mobility climate.

In reviewing the salary model, you will note there is a range of qualitative evaluations from unsatisfactory to outstanding. In the unsatisfactory column, the response is always "terminate." Unless persons whose performance is unsatisfactory are terminated, the morale consequences and development consequences to the organization will be disastrous. There is also another assumption to which your attention should be called. In the "adequate" category, salary reductions are shown. A modest salary reduction is a dramatic way to get the message to a professional whose performance is not measuring up to his capabilities. More than one salary reduction is probably good cause for termination. However, one such reduction may be just what is needed to call the person's attention to the fact that he is not achieving his goals and the goals the organization expects of him. The salary model that is shown in Appendix 2 is based upon the assumption of annual promotions and a rather quick development from new hire to the manager level. In many cases in actual practice, it takes longer than that. Accordingly, the amounts of salaries involved in the grid should be correspondingly expanded. The note to the table gives some suggestions in this regard. Now see the "how-to" reminder list in Exhibit 9 that gives you the PROFESSIONAL EXCELLENCE suggestions for creating an upward mobility climate in your organization.

Making the upward mobility climate work requires a proper atmosphere of cooperation and mutuality. Next we will discuss how to create a participative atmosphere.

EXHIBIT 9.
How to create an UPWARD MOBILITY climate with
PROFESSIONAL EXCELLENCE

1. Use the "career capability profile" (Appendix 1).

2. Make frequent small promotions.

3. Formalize the recognition and promotion process.

4. Couple promotion/recognition to salary model (Appendix 2).

5. Involve the entire professional group in the promotion/recognition process.

6. Refer to and use the professional pyramid concept in discussing and explaining the firm's policies.

CHAPTER 8

USE A PARTICIPATIVE MANAGEMENT APPROACH

A large church judicatory developed a need to bring a new sense of direction to the organization. Church leaders assigned the development of a new set of goal statements to one division of the judicatory. That division's executive retained a planning consultant to help him in the goal development process.

At first, the process seemed to go rather well. The consultant saw to it that many people in the division were involved and there was a great deal of discussion of the new goals over a one and one-half year period. When the goals were presented to the annual meeting of the judicatory, there was little discussion and the goals were ratified without any apparent dissention. For a while, it seemed, the church was well embarked in new directions.

A year later it appeared to the church leadership that little progress had actually been made in achieving the goals that had been adopted so easily a year before. After some very private discussions, some of the church leaders decided that an attitude survey was in order. Much to their surprise, the study revealed that division executives other than the one assigned to developing the goals felt they had been left out of the process entirely, as in fact they were. Since they had little sense of ownership of the new goals, the programs for which they were responsible tended to continue in the way they always had and the new goals became impossible and incapable of being achieved. The attitude study showed that the goal development process had to be started all over again because the necessary participative atmosphere had never been achieved the first time. The judiciary learned that some significant rebuilding was necessary to heal the wounds and obtain a new level of collaboration.

As we saw in Chapters 4 and 6, motivating the professional person definitely requires a sense of participation to be developed at all levels. While there are no firm rules or fixed approaches to participative management in professional organizations, there are quite a number of techniques that can be usefully employed.

As Abraham Mazlow has described in his extensive writings of "Self Actualization", motivating employees effectively means bringing responsibility to the level at which real input into the job content can be achieved. Simply pushing responsibility down, however, does not by itself achieve participation in management. To some extent, pushing responsibility down can help if it is coupled with the development of a real sense of responsibility for what is being done.

One of the easiest ways of ensuring commitment to goals for work to be done is to insist that work plans and engagements are developed from bottom-up rather than being imposed from the top. For example, it is not unusual for the account executive in charge of a particular client to say the fee for that client's work will be "so many dollars" this year. Then his people scramble around to figure out ways of achieving the goal the executive has set. A far better way of achieving participation, and better work targets, would be to ask the assistant executive and creative manager on the job to develop a proposed operating budget for that client. In developing their budget they should list the programs that will be employed and the extraordinary or, alternatively, time saving techniques they have considered in developing the budget. Then the account executive can review a work plan that has some meaning. If he disagrees, he can work to convince the assistant executive and creative manager of the changes that need to be made. This way, all parties believe when the budget is finally negotiated out that it is one in which they have confidence.

Another technique to ensure participation is using multiple involvement in performance reviews. This will be described in greater detail in Chapter 12.

Many professional organizations keep their operating results a secret. Especially in partnerships there is a sense of confidentiality that extends beyond reason. Obviously, to disclose the partners' income details to everyone including the secretaries is absurd. But disclosing periodic operating results and statistics at appropriate levels where the need to know exists can be helpful in obtaining improvements in operations and in obtaining a sense of participation. For example, the senior associates in a law firm probably should know the number of chargeable hours that are being developed on a monthly basis. Significant fluctuations from plan should be discussed openly among the management group. Another level of performance information might be the discussion of fee realization with the lawyers and associates involved in a particular client. If fee realization is less than standard, the client handling group as a whole should be responsible for working out better performance.

Building operating plans from the bottom up is probably the best way to get good plans. Some people will say it is necessary to have a statement of organizational goals before any meaningful operating plans can be developed. In fact, this is not entirely necessary although some sort of direction for the operating plans is obviously required for a start. In a typical architect and engineering firm, for example, there are several reasonable divisions of technology that would give rise to separate profit and loss statements. For example, there might be a profit and loss statement for the landscape planning division, interior design might be another, and general manufacturing plant or engineering services could be others. Each of these divisions typically would have an operating head and some key management people whose responsibility it would be to develop budgets and long-range plans for their respective divisions. In turn, the divisional budgets would be combined to produce group budgets, and then a business plan for the entire firm. The divisional leaders probably would have to involve their operating personnel in forecasting chargeable hours or billings by client and by type of work, thus ensuring by the time the firm's overall budget is put together that participation has occurred from the very bottom to the very top. Each successive level will have an opportunity to review and make changes in operating assumptions to produce a satisfactory income result.

From time to time it is useful to have feedback sessions with personnel at all levels of the organization. One way of doing this that many have found useful is the technique of a "retreat". A typical retreat might involve having all of the professional personnel of an organization leave for a weekend at some nearby secluded location. During the retreat, sessions will be held (organized on the one hand by technical discipline, and on the other hand by level of responsibility and authority) to list concerns and problems facing the organization. In successive sessions during the retreat, solutions will be developed for the problems that were identified. Finally, at the conclusion of the retreat, top management and the operating heads of the various divisions in the firm will pull together the conclusions and changes in operating plans that are produced as a result of the retreat deliberations. These are then discussed with the entire group and implementation responsibilities assigned.

Sometimes the concerns that are expressed during retreats are ridiculous to the extreme. However, having retreats enables both the ridiculous and the sensible to be brought out, discussed and disposed of in a harmonious and working atmosphere. If such outlets are not provided for professional people from time to time, they tend to seek solutions of their own, devising many that are not appropriate for the organization because they do not coincide with the organization's long-term goals or needs. The development of negotiated solutions to identified common problems among the professional group is a useful method for ensuring a high level of participation and understanding in the professional group.

Often, the top management of professional firms gets bogged down in administrative and managerial tasks. This is dangerous for two reasons. First, the leaders of professional firms typically are darn good professional performers in their own right. If a good professional gets bogged down in purely administrative tasks he tends to become frustrated and angry because the activities that he truly enjoys involving his professional skills are no longer available to him. Second, and worse, when the chief executive of a professional organization is bogged down in managerial tasks to the exclusion of all else, his people no longer see him as a viable professional in his own right. There are exceptions to this rule.

One notable apparent exception involved a large

actuarial firm which had real problems in managing itself. The firm had been founded by a very strong-minded and outstanding technician. With a firm hand he ran the company as a proprietorship for three decades. Ultimately, he died of natural causes and his son attempted to take the helm. The pressures of managing the then large firm proved to be too much for the son who died by his own hand a few years after took over the firm's operations. Then there appeared a succession of managers whose response to the firm's size and diversity was to simply let it drift. The Board of Directors decided a search for a new chief executive was in order. Unfortunately, the Board, being composed primarily of actuaries, could not agree which of them was suitably endowed to become the chief executive. Their professional jealousies were so great that not one of them could admit that another actuary had the capability of leading the firm (i.e., that the other was a superior individual). With the aid of an outside consultant, they agreed an outsider should be brought in. Ultimately, a chief executive was employed who proved to be a non-threatening figure to the members of the Board, after an agonizing search process. The pattern was established at that point for the firm's eventual decline and ultimate demise.

Obviously, there is no easy answer to problem of the type faced by the actuarial firm described above. However, with appropriate assistance, most firms can identify within their ranks, or within the profession, a technical leader who also has the necessary management skills to lead the firm. His salvation and that of the firm depends upon delegating suitably so that not all of his time is spent in managerial roles.

In an earlier chapter, there was a brief discussion of the problems involved in quality control in a professional firm. At most, a participative atmosphere is enhanced if quality control procedures are utilized to standardize output format only. The use of consulting and reviews is the best way to obtain quality control as to qualitative attributes of the firm's output. For example, quality control in a CPA firm can be achieved by appointing an acknowledged technician to the task of reviewing the reports the firm is about to release before they go into final typing. At that point, all the Q C technician can do is standardize format and make inquiries which may disclose qualitative content problems. The first line of defense is to develop an atmosphere of consultation among the partners on technical problems. If the quality control technician is brought into such consultation, output quality is usually maintained. Bureaucratic standards such as check lists and the like have some usefulness but excessive reliance on them can inhibit professional expression in quality of work.

The "stable system" is probably one of the worst things that can happen in a professional organization. It is the condition where client handling leaders develop their own cadre of professionals who are not permitted to work for any other client handling leader in the organization. As a result, the same juniors work for the same seniors and the same seniors work for the same managers and the same managers work for the same partners at all times. Thus, interaction, exchange of techniques, fair evaluation and many other desirable goals are precluded. The stable system cannot be done away with by decree. If a stable system has built up in your firm, or business organization, the only way you can break it down is by mutual agreement among the partners. This will be done for the reasons that cross-pollenization, multiplicity of work experience, fair evaluation, and so on, are desirable and necessary. Sometimes this is pretty hard to sell. In one office which I was responsible for managing, the stable system had developed to a high order before I got there.

As a result, each partner had his "favorites" and there was a highly developed sense of identity with the work done by that particular partner. It took several years to overcome the problem and it was only done by steady attrition. Some of the partners had allowed people to stay with the firm long beyond their usefulness and were suffering as a result. They had done this, of course, because they "needed" the individuals involved. What in fact has happened was that the blocking of promotion for able younger people had forced the partners operating under the stable system to rely increasingly heavily on their "over-time-in-grade" people. Fortunately, in this case, I was able to convince even the partners who had well developed "stables" that the people who should be placed outside of the organization had to go. Before I could do this I had to ensure that there was an adequate supply of quality people coming up in the firm, to assure the partners that they would have good people when they needed them. Then these partners were in a position where they needed and were able to utilize the services of other individuals who previously had been confined to working solely for other partners as well as the new high quality people who were then working their way up the organization. Gradually, an interchange began and after a few years the stable system was gone entirely. Rotating assignments is one of the best ways to avoid "stable" mentality and it is a fine way to enable a participative and mobile atmosphere.

The eight how-to steps utilized for participation in the PROFESSIONAL EXCELLENCE system are typical for most situations. There may be other steps which you can use depending on your particular situation, but use the steps suggested in Exhibit 10 as a minimum.

Next, we will cover how-to maintain continued professional development within your organization.

EXHIBIT 10
How to create a
PARTICIPATIVE ATMOSPHERE
with PROFESSIONAL EXCELLENCE

1. Develop work plans and engagement budgets from bottom up.

2. Use multiple involvement in performance reviews.

3. Disclose periodic operating results to entire organization.

4. Build operating plans from bottom up.

5. Hold retreats and feedback sessions regularly.

6. Have top management work on professional engagments, rather than purely administrative roles.

7. Utilize Q. C. to standardize output format only, relying on consultation and reviews to maintain quality of content.

8. Avoid the stable system, rotate assignments.

CHAPTER **9**

MAINTAIN CONTINUED PROFESSIONAL DEVELOPMENT

As discussed in Chapters 3 and 6, professional people are really different in that they need the personal satisfaction of continued growth in order to feel comfortable with themselves. Since personal growth is such a strong need demonstrated by professionals, it makes sense to respond in a well planned and structured way. Unfortunately, despite the existence of such a need, if left to chance many professionals will simply fail to take the initiative their expressed desires would imply one should expect. This is not an indictment of the need, merely a recognizable human failing. Personal development is too easily put off when the pressures of client services provide easy excuses. As a result, self-help courses and home study are usually not satisfactory substitutes for formal outside training in professional development.

With the advent of CPE (Continued Professional Education) requirements for certain professions, a whole new industry has sprung up almost overnight to meet the legislated requirements imposed upon accountants, physicians and others. An interesting development in observing this new industry, is the extent to which purely technical courses are overwhelmed by formal education in all types of managerial and personal development.

In some firms, the cost of technical education has become absolutely enormous. The rapid evolution of accounting theory, for example, imposes a significant cost in reeducating people in all levels every single year. Thus, in such environments there is usually a built-in need for continued development programs of at least the technical type and, as a consequence, there is a tendency for economic reasons to limit them to just technical subjects. A practical way to maintain the aura of personal choice in these situations is to take the attitude that, "it is a given that everyone will participate, now let's talk about your selection this year!" Obviously, the continued professional education programs required by licensing boards will solve many of the problems in the "given."

In one case where the long-range development of a professional practice was involved, agreement was reached among the partners that promotion criteria would include successful completion of a "Winning With People" course* for one level and a broader management development course for the next level. In this case, no one had heard of the "winning with people" course, but many of the partners had read books like "I'm OK, You're OK" and were aware of the concepts involved. They readily agreed that teaching their seniors how to understand and employ "win-win" techniques would be useful for their later development. Sometimes, if queried effectively by management, middle and lower level professionals will directly or indirectly suggest useful development courses for the firm's

---

* Addison-Wesley Publishing Co., Boston.

use. This is a good way to ensure participation and will enable top management to learn more of what is really wanted by their people.

To limit the development system to purely technical education, fails to capitalize on the opportunity for enhancing real personal growth and for meeting strong personal needs. Professional development should be balanced among:

Technical— updates on new theory, rules, laws or other basic skills.

Managerial— developing and understanding management skills and theory.

Personal— enhancing such abilities such as speaking, writing and time organizing.

There are some very good courses available outside of the CPE system which you may wish to consider. In addition to the "Winning With People" material that can be purchased and utilized by your own personnel, you should consider some of the following:

1. The Xerox sales course — teaches the concepts of matching feature to benefit to need so that sales strategy can be directed to the customers real or perceived needs.

2. John J. McCarthy's sales strategy system—Professional Salesmanship Center, 1221 Avenue of the Americans, N.Y., N.Y. 10020 teaches an organized and analytical approach to estimating the selling situation, gathering intelli-

gence, analyzing need and reacting to it in a professional fashion.

3. Toastmasters — an international organization of voluntary group meetings that teaches effective personal speaking techniques and provides plenty of practice to reverse the "nervous stomach" that most of us have when speaking before a group.

4. Dale Carnegie Institute — courses on personal motivation and growth, available in most large cities.

There are also numerous managerial and communication courses offered within the CPE educational system. If you are not receiving catalogs by direct mail (the most frequent form of solicitation) consider dropping a note to The American Management Association in New York or one of the various commercial education firms now in the business such as AIM International, Inc. Contact your own profession's state society for information on their offerings.

In the PROFESSIONAL EXCELLENCE system there are four principal "how-to" steps as set forth in Exhibit 11. Obviously, you will want to meet or exceed the CPE requirements for your particular profession. You can use extra CPE and related training as special rewards to outstanding people. If utilized properly, the relieving of a key senior or associate for example, from duties for an extra three day period will probably not hurt the firm's output significantly but will be well recognized by that individual's peer group as something special which he has earned. When you develop your own career capability profile, you may want to put certain special courses as requirements for entry into the next level. Since technical training is probably a given, you may end up using enhancement of personal skills as the factor for entry into the next level.

EXHIBIT 11
How to maintain
CONTINUED PROFESSIONAL
DEVELOPMENT
WITH PROFESSIONAL EXCELLENCE

1. Meet or exceed CPE* requirements for formal technical education.

2. Award extra CPE or equivalent courses as special rewards to outstanding people.

3. Utilize management development, sales training, personal skills training as requirements in the career capability system.

4. Use the "counselor system" to assure proper guidance is given to people at all levels.

*CPE — Continued Professional Education, requirements now enacted by legislation for professional licensing in many states for a number of profesional disciplines (particularly accounting, psychology, medicine).

Another part of the development system with PRO-FESSIONAL EXCELLENCE should be the use of a "counselor system" in which every individual in your organization is assigned to another individual at the next higher level for personal counseling on continued professional development. Typically, the counselor system is installed with the higher level individual being given the personal responsibility for the continued development for four or five persons immediately below him in rank. In addition to the ongoing guidance of the counselees on professional development in a formal sense, counselors can participate in performance reviews and obtain an expanded role in developing the firm's management techniques themselves. Regular use of the career capability profile and similar guidelines as reference will help the counselors and counselees to seek assignments, educational and outside activities that enhance the individual counselee's personal growth. In some firms, the counselor system is developed as sort of an "ombudsman" to "fight for the rights" of the counselees. This is not particularly healthy in that it assumes that an antagonistic or combative environment is necessary for proper development. Better yet, use the counselor system as a means of training the counselors in what is expected of people at all levels of the institution and ensuring that the counselees have somebody with their personal interests foremost in mind. The counselor system will also help overcome the tendency on the part of very young people in the organization to feel that they are not cared for and are merely ciphers in a list. Counselors will also be committed to desirable behavioral and development characteristics by the act of guiding their counselees in positive ways and toward firm goals. They can't reject for themselves what they are teaching to others.

With PROFESSIONAL EXCELLENCE, these factors are integrated into an overall system that reinforces itself. Up to this point, we have developed how-to steps for maintaining upward mobility, participative management, and continued professional development. Each one of the sub-systems involved in these steps is integrated with one and another. For example, the career capability profile gives guidance to the counselors on what should be expected of people at each level. In turn, counselors guide the individuals for whom they are responsible in seeking to achieve these attributes. The participative system in which the attributes are identified and developed enhances the overall health of the organization.

The next step in the PROFESSIONAL EXCELLENCE system is to define responsibilities and levels within the organization.

CHAPTER 10

DEFINE RESPONSIBILITIES AND LEVELS

As we all know, a number of professions are undergoing major changes at this time. In addition to the accounting and legal professions which are learning how to "sell", other professions are having similar changes. An interesting case involves the branch office of an advertising and marketing service firm, the headquarters of which are located in a large industrial city. To diversify, the management of the firm decided to open branch offices in several other cities, including one in Houston. Allowing only skimpy resources, they assigned one of their brightest young technicians to the new Houston office together with a cadre of approximately four people. Their first job was to service an existing client using the new Houston resources on existing business. After the office had been open for a few months, instructions came from headquarters that the local in charge executive should start selling services to potential new clients. He was asked to "get his people out on the road." Because he and his people were technically oriented, there was fear and resistance to these new instructions. After a few months of no progress, the branch executive was called on the carpet by headquarters for his "non-compliance" and was told to do it or else. He went back home in a state of paralysis. Not only did service to the existing clientele in Houston suffer, but the attitudes of all the other people in the office were affected as well. Finally, the executive left the firm and went into private practice on his own.

What was the failure here? Actually, there were probably several failures. First, the firm selected a technically oriented individual who was capable of rendering service at the level their clients needed, but had no training or background in expanding that service. He also had no managerial background. But, the primary failure was the fact that his responsibilities and level of performance had not been clearly defined before he accepted the assignment. Thus, neither he nor his superiors knew what to expect from him. Since the office had been opened with much hope, the expectations were larger than reality should have permitted. As a result, when the branch executive was chastised for his non-performance, he did not know what was expected of him. Further, he had no training or background to do what was needed.

The PROFESSIONAL EXCELLENCE management approach involves integrating, in many ways, a cohesive and interdependent system. A key aspect of this system is the use of well defined ranks or levels within the organization. As mentioned above, the use of frequent small promotion recognizes what happens in real life as people change in their abilities and scope of experience. Identifying what is expected at various levels makes sense in any organization. No two organizations are exactly alike but there are some great similarities among professional firms in the same business and there are more similarities among various professions than you would normally expect might be the case.

Refererence to the career capability profile gives

some indication of the types of levels that would make sense in a typical accounting firm. Combining these identified levels with an evaluation grid system (see salary model in Exhibit 2) gives rise to further integration of the system.

Surprising as it may seem, by far the majority of professional firms and organizations do not have written definitions of responsibility for all levels in the organization. Typically, there will be some written job descriptions for clerical and administrative personnel but it is unlikely that you will find the comprehensive job descriptions for other levels in the organization, unless the firm is well advanced and has people in charge who really enjoy the process of management for its own sake. Even firms whose professional abilities require them to recommend job descriptions and definitions to their clients sometimes do not have them for their own organization. Since this requirement is so easily accomplished, it seems almost unnecessary to suggest it. The simple fact is, however, that PROFESSIONAL EXCELLENCE will not work unless there is some agreement among people at all levels as to the range of responsibilities to which they can be held.

There is an additional technique involved in PROFESSIONAL EXCELLENCE which I have utilized successfully based upon years of experience in managing professionals. This technique involves allowing relatively full disclosure of the permissable salary levels within the organization. It is an old saw that "salaries are confidential, but everyone knows what everyone else is paid." This may not be true in some professional firms, but is generally true for quite a number of them. It is difficult to escape the fact that bright people can figure for themselves what various levels approximate, given starting salaries for new people. If everyone is involved in the recruiting process, it is almost impossible to avoid disclosure of starting salaries.

Therefore, since salary information is generally known, at least to some extent, it makes sense to capitalize on the situation and convert disclosure of pay ranges by level and the differentiation for outstanding work to a positive and morale building approach in managing the professional person. In my experience it is a positive and useful tactic to disclose the salary model to all professional personnel. The model may not necessarily disclose compensation at the partner or owner level of the firm but, to be useful, it should disclose ranges for everything up to that point.

One reaction to this philosophy, before it is actually employed in a firm, is concern that a grid system might bureaucratize the firm into an immobile network. The normal fear is that individuals in the professional firm will be demotivated by disclosure of a system. Experience shows the contrary to be true.

The key is to use open discussion during implementation and to show the individual how he can make the system work for himself. Further, with the system having relatively frequent promotions (as described in Chapter 7) the individual who is performing well will have frequent confirmation of his progress. Those who are not doing well, who are not well rounded or who are not performing in one aspect or another of their professional expertise become aware of these facts sooner in the PROFESSIONAL EXCELLENCE system because they will miss the promotions that should be coming along on a regular basis. Many of them will take corrective action, given adequate guidance.

Another concern is that people will become lock-stepped into a promotion network that sets up excessive expectations. This is overcome, in fact, by the differences between individuals. It might take one lawyer a year and half to move from new hire to junior associate whereas it might take another lawyer two to three years to accomplish the same level of responsibility.

Since such individual differences are bound to exist, the "lock-stepped" time-in-grade philosophy can usually be overcome rather easily. In all your discussions with your people, during reviews, at retreats, and other occasions it is useful to emphasize that the system is not rigid and permits promotion based upon performance rather than time.

Another benefit of having well defined responsibility definitions tied in with your career capability profile is the fact that people who are not performing are identified sooner and moved out before too long a stagnation occurs.

This overcomes another typical problem in the non-managed professional organization. We all know the old timer who can not quite seem to make it happen well enough for a promotion, but who has been around long enough to become an institution in the firm. The longer he stays around the more difficult it will be place him outside the firm. Yet, probably the best thing for the old timer is to put him in a situation where his goals and realistic aspirations can be achieved rather than leaving him in a situation where he is inevitably compared to the "movers and shakers" that are moving up rapidly in the firm. It may not seem possible, but I have had the enviable record of almost never (see one major exception below) having "fired" anyone in some twenty-four years of professional firm management. This resulted from enabling people who were not making it to move at their own schedule to positions outside of the firm where their goals and aspiration could be best achieved. This condition had many desirable side benefits. it enabled the departing persons to go out with their "heads held high." This, in turn, caused people remaining to believe they would be treated fairly and would have the same opportunities if they needed them. Finally, it created a large and loyal alumni group

EXHIBIT 12

How to DEFINE
RESPONSIBILITIES and LEVELS
with
PROFESSIONAL EXCELLENCE

1. Using participative techniques, prepare written responsibility definitions for all levels.

2. Allow full disclosure of the salary matrix (see Appendix 2).

3. Avoid disclosure of individual's compensation.

4. Make full use of the carrer capability profile.

who actively promoted the best interests of the firm, hundreds of effective salesmen!

It may not seem obvious, but disclosure of individuals' specific compensation is to be discouraged at all costs. In one office to which I was moved during my career as a managing partner, I quickly learned that the staff had developed a technique for finding out how well they were doing. Annually, the key people in the organization would meet a neighborhood bar and would compare W-2 forms to determine what recognition had been given. Since there were no defined levels of responsibility and since performance reviews were infrequent, if ever, comparing W-2 forms was the only way the people could find out where they stood. This put some of the younger and more able people into rather embarassing positions because, in addition to the other problems, the office did not have a well defined salary structure and system. Thus, some of the younger people were getting paid more than some of the more experienced people, with attendant dismay and disarray on the part of all. As much as I dislike arbitrary and finite "orders" I passed word to the staff that the next person found disclosing or asking for salary information from another would not even have to stop by my office to pick up his last paycheck. The implication, of course, was that he would be gone so fast it would make his head swim. It fortunately happened that one of the more agressive individuals involved in this practice of the W-2 swapping was one who should have been placed outside of the organization long ago. Therefore, when the opportunity presented itself, I used his dismissal as an example to the rest of the organization and the problem quickily disappeared forever.

PROFESSIONAL EXCELLENCE depends upon the integration of these job definitions with actual practice. The next step is to demonstrate an understanding of the roles your people play in their various positions in the organization.

CHAPTER 11

UNDERSTAND THE ROLES YOUR PEOPLE PLAY

A large international advertising firm had evolved some strange titles for its chief executive group that did not correspond to the actual roles the individuals played in managing the firm. The man with the Chief Executive title was, in reality, retired and merely served to carry the firm name in a ceremonial way. The president had the title of chief operating officer but was, in fact, the chief executive in that his province was primarily policy determination. Day to day management of the firm rested in a senior executive who had the inappropriate title of Assistant to the President. Unfortunately, the Chairman and the President were lulled into believing that the Assistant to the President had a level of importance equal to that of his title, rather than his real role in the firm. After several years of waiting for the Chairman to retire and hoping that his title would be made to correspond to the real role he carried in the firm, the Assistant to the President decided to take early retirement and pursue other business interests. He had grown tired of waiting and believed he was carrying the entire load. The situation was all the more unfortunate because shortly after the Assistant to the President retired, people in the organization started calling him for advice and assistance on day to day operating matters, which help he was not in a position to give any more. Soon, things began to come unglued and the loss of several clients occurred before the board of directors recognized that a real chief operating officer was needed.

The leadership group in a professional service organization usually has a fairly good idea of its role in dealing with clients and the community, the above example notwithstanding. But, in many cases the individuals' understandings of the roles that should be played by the client, the key account handling executive and others in their organization vary widely. They depend in many cases, as one would expect, upon variations in the personal background of the individuals involved. This lack of uniformity in what usually is a fairly flat organization structure can limit the firm's ability to utilize the pulling power of positive motivation. PROFESSIONAL EXCELLENCE will not work well where roles are not understood. A lack of uniformity and understanding can also prevent the use of another technique for quality control in personal development called the "colleague system" that is introduced later in this chapter.

First, let us briefly examine some of the roles that should be understood. Following are some typical responses various role holders will give when asked what are the business needs of their position:

Client

— Do my engagement completely and well

— Help me personally and help my company

— Charge a reasonable fee

— Provide <u>all</u> services I need

Professional superior

— Control and complete the work

— Maintain quality

— Keep me informed, no surprises!

— Help our staff grow

Professional subordinate

— Train me

— Help me grow

— Give me feedback

— Tell others how good I am

Who are all these admonitions directed to?

They are addressed to the key account handling executive. That person will vary according to the structure and personality of the particular professional organization. In some cases it may be a young partner, in other cases it may be an account executive, in others it will be an associate, still others will have the manager, etc., depending upon the titles the firm uses and the nature of the firm's business. The response of the key account handling executive when presented with some of the above demands is to feel overwhelmed, especially where there is a lack of general understanding of roles in the organization. Two things need to be done.

First, develop an organization profile of your key client account handling executive. It is less important where this level exists in your organization than whether there are enough of them and their roles are well enough understood that all the clients whom you intend to serve can be effectively provided with the service they need.

Second, an understanding of the key man role should be demonstrated and discussed openly and fully at management meetings, development seminars and retreat sessions. Not only should the key executive's role be discussed and understood, but the roles of subordinates and the client should be reviewed and examined regularly. These roles need to be discussed repeatedly and the understanding demonstrated by top management so that when crises and problems take place there is almost a "knee-jerk" reaction in selecting who is dispatched to take care of the situation and how he responds to it. If participative approaches are used in settling on organizational roles, better understanding is more likely to be accomplished for there will be opportunities to develop responses to the real needs of the firm's key managers. This means that interaction is the most useful part of the approach. The discussion of how to develop a participative climate in Chapter 8 outlines the types of participative approaches you can use.

One technique I use in teaching management development courses to professional firm executives is to stratify the group according to their respective levels in their own organizations. Then each group is asked to define how it sees its role in its organization. The responses are often quite uniform and in contrast interestingly as the various levels are compared. This technique can be carried one step further by having each stratified sub-group list in priority order what they consider to be the main responsibilities of the level both above them and immediately below them.

We have often heard the aphorism "sending a boy to do a man's job" and sometimes the aphorism is expressed the other way around. If the role listing exercise is performed at a retreat, for example, you will have adequate time to explore the differences in perception between various levels about specific roles within the organization. The "man's job" will be better understood. See Exhibit 13 for an example of how a subordinate and a manager view the manager's role differently. The differences need to be negotiated out so there is a uniform understanding throughout the organization.

Simultaneously you should assign other senior executives in your organization to act as colleagues on each client. See Exhibit 14 for definition of the colleague's responsibilities in a typical professional firm. Determining who the colleague should be and who the key executive should be will depend upon the facts in the client situation. For example, a strong continuity and contact needs would indicate that the person who first sold the job (sometimes an euphumism like "brought in the contact" are used to put a polite aura around the real thing) would be assigned as the key executive. In another situation where technical requirements are more important than the original client contact you might assign as the key account handling executive a technically oriented person who could meet the client service needs, with the colleague role being assigned to the person who brought in the work.

The assignment of an active colleague to provide another dimension to the client handling relationship really works. In a "buddy system" way the colleague and key manager work jointly to ensure the client's needs are fully met. Larger client requirements may cause the colleague to be virtually as fully involved as the key account handling executive. Sometimes technical requirements cause the colleague to handle some aspects of the work on a line basis, in which case the key account handling executive oversees planning, timeliness, fulfillment of commitments and other non-technical parts of the relationship. An example in a law firm will be to have the litigation partner handling a particular case on a line basis for a client assigned to a general corporate matters partner as key man. In a CPA firm an audit partner colleague working for the tax colleague who brought in the client would make sense where an annual examination of the client's financial statements was also involved.

Sometimes the initial reaction to the use of a colleague system might be a concern that the roles of the various levels of personnel involved in supplying professional service to the client will be cluttered. In actual practice, the colleague system has proved to be a useful approach many more times than it has not. It can be especially useful in helping the account executive or key manager in balancing the priorities set by the various (sometimes simultaneous) demands he is typically called upon to perform. As such, it helps demonstrate the entire organizations's better understanding of roles and ability to provide a high level of client service.

Demonstration of the awareness of roles can be carried out in the process of negotiating uniform role definitions for all other levels once the key client handling executive level is identified. It is often amazing to me how many professional firms do not formally go through the process of identifying who has the key client handling responsibility. You can overcome confusion among your people and provide a higher level of client service by using this PROFESSIONAL EXCELLENCE technique to ensure everyone understands what his responsibilities are.

Finally, in order to make sure that roles are understood, and as a back-up to assure that client service is provided at the levels your firm requires, a periodic client service review is a good idea. In my organization we used to insist the colleague conduct an independent client satisfaction meeting with the client's chief executive at least once a year. The information gathered at that meeting would then be utilized in client service planning for the ensuing year. Often, we would find that additional work is needed to meet the clients' service needs. By bringing the results of the client satisfaction meeting to the service planning activity, we could ensure that the client was getting all the work he requested. This has a neat attribute besides the role definition characteristics it provides. By having a client satisfaction meeting periodically, almost invariably additional work is requested by the client, a lot easier way to obtain new business than going out and "foot-soldiering" for new clients.

The next aspect of the integration of the PROFESSIONAL EXCELLENCE system is tying well structured performance appraisals to the parts of the system we now have developed.

EXHIBIT 13
SAMPLE LISTS OF ROLES
(taken from a typical feedback session)

I. Subordinate's Perspective of a Manager's Role

— Resource for answers to questions   *
— Organization of work required to meet deadlines
— Telling what to do and why
— Feeedback on how I'm doing

OR

— Supervisor of field work (getting the job done by planning and reviewing)
— Staff development
— Communication (supportive relationship between the senior and the manager)
— Performance review (letting the senior know how he's doing
— Collection of fees   *
— New business development

II. Manager's Perspective of His role

— Responsibility to get the job done—with high quality and within the budget
— Leadership role
— Training of assistants within the amount of time relevant to the budget
— Self-development in order to become a manager
— Practice development (everybody's business, though not in all offices)

OR

— Planning
— Technical review and job supervision
— Communication (clients, among ourselves)
— Education and training of staff (our self-development)
— Profitability
— New business development
— Personnel counseling   *

* Areas where differences in perspective exist — these must be negotiated out and uniform understandings developed.

77

EXHIBIT 14
Colleague responsibilities typically assigned in a professional firm

1. Consult with account handling executive on all matters requested by either the client or the account handling executive.

2. Review all reports rendered to the client

3. Participate in client service reviews and client service planning.

4. Review all budgets for work to be done for the client.

5. Consult on assignments of personnel.

6. Conduct an independent client satisfaction meeting with client chief executive.

7. Assist account handling executive whenever requested and provide back-up in case of his absence to ensure continued service to the client.

EXHIBIT 15
How to UNDERSTAND ROLES in the PROFESSIONAL EXCELLENCE system

1. Develop an organization profile of the key client handling executive.*

2. Negotiate uniform role definitions for other levels.

3. For training, back-up and quality control use a "colleague system".

4. Demonstrate awareness of roles in client responsibilities.

5. Use a periodic client service review to reinforce understood roles (and to ensure each client is receiving the service he requires on a well planned basis).

* tie this role definition into the career capability profile.

CHAPTER 12

EMPLOY WELL STRUCTURED APPRAISALS

As Sam Johnson is reputed to have said, "he who praises everybody, praises nobody".

In an earlier chapter I described the personnel handling partner in a large professional service firm who was generally regarded as being a "good guy". Yet, one of his major characteristics was the fact that he could never give anyone bad news. As a result, the people for whom he had responsibility were constantly in a quandry as to where they stood and where they were going. This personnel handling partner was selected for his job because he was perceived as being a "good guy" while in his anxiety to tell people what he thought they wanted to hear as opposed to what they needed to know, he really undermined the entire fabric of the organization.

We find Sam Johnson's statement easy to agree with, yet one common characteristic of many performance appraisal systems, in practice, is the coupling of mild praise with no specifics. This often happens even though there is a desperate need of both the appraiser and the appraised for some form of agreement and some specifics in their relationship. One of the most important factors in managing professional people is a working performance appraisal system.

Some of the characteristics of good appraisal systems are:

— *all parties are well prepared*

— *honesty prevails*

— *specifics abound*

— *constructive approaches are used*

— *agreement to a plan of action is* <u>*key*</u>

On the other hand, appraisal efforts which are not effective usually include some of the following:

— *unprepared participants*

— *one or more individuals being late*

— *indifferent attitudes*

— *surprises*

— *one way communications or lecturing*

— *lack of commitments or agreement*

The obvious objective of an appraisal interview is to set the stage for the appraised individual's further performance and personal growth. This can best be done in a conversational atmosphere. One way I have found of accomplishing the proper conversational atmosphere is to use at least two reviewers on one reviewee. This forces the discussion into a conversational mode. One person may disagree with the other from time to time or may take the side of one or another participant without destroying the progress of the discussion. Concerns about being "ganged-up upon" do not manifest themselves in actual practice if your two reviewers are properly coached and prepared.

The prime purpose is, of course, to set the stage for

future development of the entire organization. Thus, the objectives of the interview must be well understood by the participants before the interview takes place. The interview must lead in the direction that has been charted for the firm.

Another benefit from double teaming is the ability it provides you to train younger members of your executive group in the process of making sure the individual's goals coincide with the needs of the firm. Also, by having some of your middle management executives participate in appraisal interviews while you are present, they will be making commitments to "their" interviewee that they cannot back down upon when it comes time for their own performance evaluation.

Often, we hear that appraisal interviews consist of one executive sitting down with another and saying "Well, Harry, what did you do wrong last year"? Even if that is not what they actually say, sometimes the impression is given that such is what they mean. Use of the PROFESSIONAL EXCELLENCE career capability profile as an example in describing stages in career development will help to ensure the individual's goals are made to coincide with the needs of the organization. And, the "what did you do wrong" question does not need to be asked, because the entire focus should be forward. Since double teaming enables the lead member of the team to train the counselor or second member in interview and guidance techniques, it also helps to avoid miscues and misunderstandings. In my experience in turning around a professional service firm, I have found sitting in as a team member in key appraisals to be a major tool in redirecting the organization.

As much as two sets of interviews, each six months apart, may be necessary to get the redirection process started.

Often, coaching sessions for every interviewer just

prior to starting a round of interviews are useful in setting the stage and in revalidating previously trained techniques.

Of course, it is almost impossible to have meaningful reviews without well documented personnel files. If appraisals are planned for six months' intervals, then written performance reports are needed for every assignment of every professional in the organization. Appendix 3 shows a typical appraisal evaluation report that I have found to be useful in a number of different types of professional firms. Even though it is titled an engagement performance review form it is useful for both annual and semi-annual reviews as well.

Generally, the shorter the interval for periodic appraisal reviews, the more important it is to have written performance reports for every assignment. It is always important to have documented performance reports, no matter what the review interval is. If the organization is really going to perform in an outstanding manner, then support and clerical personnel cannot be excepted. It matters little what "form" is used since there are so many acceptable types. Usually, however, it means more to the people filling out written reports if they have had a hand in designing the report they are using. This leads to using care in introducing or modifying "canned" forms so as to avoid the perception that they are being "handed down" to the organization. If the tools your people are using are perceived to be a product of their attitudes and needs they will accept them more readily.

Just as every meeting or negotiation must end in agreement of some sort to be useful to the participants, every performance review must do so as well. In terms of our friend "Harry" from the statement above, the best results will be obtained by the retorical "Harry, what are we going to do to help each other to continue our growth"? If such a commitment does not happen it could mean a number of things:

1. The appraiser was poorly prepared for the interview,

2. The firm's directions and goals, and thus the directions for the individual, are unclear, or

3. The individual has run out of capacity or desire for further commitment.

Even in the third case, agreement can and must be reached. Possibly the answer is the firm should help the individual recharge his batteries so further commitment can be obtained. Alternatively, the firm should help him obtain employment where his goals coincide with his new employers' needs. In any case, some form of agreement should be reached. The actions necessary in possibilities one and two, above, should be obvious. In that case, the job of correcting deficiencies is yours as chief executive.

In my experience, where adequate performance reviews have not been going on for some period of time it will take the chief executive almost full time for several years to get the system turned around properly. In one large consulting firm, I recommended the chief executive work on appraisals and employee interviews sixty percent of his available time for a full year. It is necessary for him to personally interview and document the results with every individual in the organization before he could start effectively relating those individuals goals to the partners' definition of the organization's objectives.

In the PROFESSIONAL EXCELLENCE system, there is almost nothing as important as the well structured appraisal. With the other tools that have been described in chapters 7 through 11, you have an integrated employee motivation and measurement system that will enable you to direct the organization most effectively.

The final steps in earning more through the use of PROFESSIONAL EXCELLENCE, now that you have your employee management systems in place, is to start working on practice development, recruiting and the business plan. Practice development is next.

EXHIBIT 16
How to obtain
WELL STRUCTURED APPRAISALS
with PROFESSIONAL EXCELLENCE

1. Have appraisals at regular intervals for all personnel.

2. Use dual-teaming to ensure thorough discussion and to train team members.

3. Make sure all participants are well prepared in advance.

4. Document all matters discussed.

5. Insist on specific agreements being reached and documented.

6. Utilize appraisals as the primary tool for relating individuals' goals to the needs of the organization.

7. Have well documented personnel files with periodic performance reports performed for every one in the organization.

CHAPTER 13

TREAT PRACTICE DEVELOPMENT AS A REGULAR THING

Just the other day in Detroit, something happened that would have curled the hair of professional people even a year or two ago. It seems that the city audit was up for "bid". The city, which had not been audited for several years, found itself in need of an outside audit to help improve its sagging bond ratings and the audit department was charged with the responsibility of making the selection. One firm, which had a traditionally strong relationship with the city auditor's department submitted the low bid and an action plan promising to do all kinds of good things in training the city auditors up to a professional level. Up to that point, everything seemed ordinary.

Then the dam broke. A competing firm whose proposal had not been accepted sent one of its partners around to the city council, one by one, lobbying on behalf of his firm. His objective was to convince the city council that his firm had a more effective affirmative action program than the firm recommended by the city audit department. This had never happened before, and the council, taken aback by the agressive approach, decided to table the whole matter. Lo and behold! Another firm stepped into the void and in a week's time prepared and submitted a third proposal that promised to do the work for less money and promised to tie-in with the local black-owned CPA firm. That took the wind out of the sails of the previous two firms and city council picked the third firm.

This type of direct and overt marketing would never have happened several years ago. Pressure from the FTC, Congress and numerous other sources have forced CPAs into agressively marketing their services in a way that would not have been dreamed of in past years.

One of life's seeming mysteries is the tendency of so many professional people to want to "do their own thing" through a purely technical role in life and, thus, to not expose themselves to possible rejection by attempting to sell their services. We have seen how this naturally falls from the human needs of the types of people who make good professionals. In my experience, this aversion to selling also is due to a misunderstanding about what effective selling is really all about. Hucksterism, hard selling (of the type described above) and forcing one's self upon a hapless customer is usually just as ineffective in marketing professional services as it is in other segments of industry, probably more. The key to effective professional selling is identifying a client need and making sure that you and your firm have the services to meet that need. Often, effective selling can be made much easier by good strategic planning.

For example, some years ago I was in a situation where a declining client base due to death and attrition among the firm's typical small-business clientele had created a grim forecast through the next few years. An opportunity presented itself in doing some specialized medicare audits. We had to make the decision as to whether a less than normal fee would be taken for this government work and a great deal of thought went into our strategy. After giving it considerable evaluation, the partners decided that they would obtain the medicare work at almost any "cost." Our strategy was based on the fact that, until that point in time, health care institutions had not been audited by CPA firms to anywhere near the extent that commercial and industrial concerns had been audited. With increasing government control and intervention in the health care industry, we concluded that it was only a matter of time before the entire health care system would be forced to undergo periodic examination of financial statements just like the rest of industry. Effective selling in this case depended upon the overall strategic plan.

As it turned out over the next five years, the plan worked marvelously. The medicare examinations gave us the opportunity to get into numerous health care institutions that had never been audited before. Through the medicare work we developed an expertise in the terminology and cost reimbursements concepts necessary to be able to help the hospitals in obtaining the highest dollar of revenue from the government supported patients they were obliged to take. Thus, it was only a matter of time before an experienced cadre of personnel had become personally knowledgable about the industry and personally known to many of the industry's local leaders. Within a few more years, the firm was the acknowledged leader in health care work in its area. In fact, it came to the point where other firms would not compete because of their perception that our firm simply knew too much about health care work for the other firms to have any credibility at all. This became a self-fulfilling prophecy that enhanced the original investment many times over.

Once upon a time there were serious and important ethical constraints on selling by professional people. To some extent, these constraints still exist in medicine and allied professions. Because of its relatively high visibility, the accounting profession has probably led all of the other professions in the breakdown of the traditional ethical virtues. Where, once upon a time, it was forbidden to approach another firm's client, it is now no longer so in both accounting and a number of other professions. Not too many years ago, several states had laws which prohibited professionals from competing on the basis of price. In fact it was an act contrary to law in some places to submit a hourly fee estimate that was less than "customary." In some cases, state laws prohibited a professional from accepting an engagement where the prior professional had not, in fact, already been terminated by the client. Virtually all of these laws have broken down or have been struck down.

The prohibition against advertising has been virtually eliminated both in accounting and the law. Thus, we have seen some ludicrous displays as people have experimented with their new found freedoms. I know of one case where an accounting firm is the laughing stock of its city because of its tombstone advertisements saying "you know where the professionals are" and the word on the street among bankers and lawyers is that the professionals, in this case, are in most of the other firms than the one carrying the advertisement! The funny little man on TV that comes popping up out of the swimming pool with a billboard emblazoned on his hairy chest in another example of excesses, except this time he is a lawyer. These things will simmer down in due course and some modicum of decorum will be found for professional selling and advertising. In my view, advertising by professions should not extend beyond appropriate telephone listings and modest tombstone type announcements of the existence of services or specialties which can, in fact, be demonstrated by personal expertise. Also, I predict that price competition will ultimately be recognized by most potential clients to be self-defeating. Sensible clients have long since realized that they get what they pay for if they have a good and well understood relationship with their professional firm, no matter what discipline is involved.

Some of the principles involved in selling professional work include the following. First, practice development is a personal thing. In professional work, selling involves obtaining the confidence of the client and this can only be done by consistently demonstrating that you and your firm can meet the client's needs and by showing an understanding and experience with the types of services he requires. This can best be accomplished by building personal confidence and confidence in the person through continued exposure.

The same skills that are useful in life are useful in business selling. Effective marketers do not turn on like a light bulb. People who write and speak well will naturally do better than those who do not. But, these skills can be trained. People who listen well, too, will do better than all. This skill is also trainable. So, train yourself and your people!

We need to recognize that skills can be developed more in some persons than in others. Most of the needed skills for effective selling are developable. Consider the Xerox sales training methodology referred to in a previous chapter. Matching feature to benefit to need works in a professional service as well as in hard goods, perhaps even better. McCarthy's sales strategy analysis, also described above, works and can be easily trained. Dual teaming is a good obvious technique to improve effectiveness and institutionalize training by example. Dual teaming also is very effective in facilitating the psychological transference of confidence and loyalty from the leader or contact originator to the junior member of the team in the client's eyes.

Community service is often regarded as a place where professional people can meet potential clients. What most professional people fail to recognize, however, is that community service has an entirely different and very useful benefit. By building community service into your organization plan (see the career capability profile) you can expose younger people to taking risks in organization management. Testing and developing interpersonal skills is enhanced where the risk of failure is not the sacrifice of a career. For years I have used the technique of introducing modern management techniques into community organizations as an advertisement for my firm's skills. Both as a training device for younger people and as an advertising technique for demonstrating expertise, community service works. And, to some extent, community activities still remain a good way to meet and interact with other business people.

Marketing should be part of everyone's role in the organization. Some firms mistakenly let a few "outside" partners do all the "selling." This approach appears (at least on the surface) to comfort the individuals who want a purely technical role. But, it carries the seed of its own defeat in that it eventually causes the rainmakers (as one law firm called the more outgoing of its partners) to pass on, and often before they have started new growth of needed skills within the firm. A hundred people, each doing something in their own most effective way, are infinitely more productive than a few rainmakers. Sometimes merely recognizing that there must be multiple contacts with the "outside world" will help break the issue into the open so it can be dealt within your firm.

In the PROFESSIONAL EXCELLENCE system, use of the career capability profile and definition of responsibilities ties the ordinary need for selling into each appropriate level in the organization. The expectation and intensity of selling efforts escalates gradually through the professional's career.

The nine "how-to" points in Exhibit 17 are useful

reminders of how to make practice development a regular thing. Next, we cover how to make sure you have the right people.

EXHIBIT 17
How to treat
PRATICE DEVELOPMENT as a
regular thing with
PROFESSIONAL EXCELLENCE

1. Employ everyone in the organization in P.D. — many are more effective than one.

2. Professional selling is a personal thing, make appropriate exposure a part of each persons' goals.

3. Use specific skills development (XEROX selling course, for example) to break barriers down.

4. Encourage people to use their best skills, (writing in one, speaking in another) rather than expecting everyone to be perfect.

5. Use community service for dual purposes, risk-free management training <u>and</u> exposure to other leaders in a positive way.

6. Have specific targets planned.

7. Prepare a strategic market plan as a part of the firm's business plan.

8. Use price competition selectively, for it can only hurt in the long run.

9. Dual team and carefully analyze all new situations.

USE STRATEGIC HIRING PRACTICES

Some years ago, in the situation in which I was providing consultation on developing a firm management system to a large professional organization, I noticed their partner income was significantly lower than what should have been expected for an organization of their size in their profession. Further inquiry developed a number of factors that explained this situation. First, the firm had no really viable business plan, although the partners had made an effort to develop some directions for their practice. The "plan" lacked a cohesive forward structure for personnel. In fact, they did not have hardly any of the key "how-to" steps shown in Exhibit 18. As a consequence, their personnel pyramid was too flat for the type of business they were in and they were having difficulty supervising a fairly large group of younger people.

The most important failing, however, was the fact that, in an effort to improve the partner's income, the firm had embarked on a program of hiring less than the most able new personnel. Their ostensible objective was to reduce operating costs, and thus (hopefully) increase the partner's income. In fact, this step produced exactly the opposite result. By hiring less than the very best people, the firm had committed itself to compensation, and thus billing rates, that were less than prevailed in the community. While this might have had a beneficial short-term effect, the long-term consequences had become readily apparent as the company's billing rates and work quality showed the effects of employing less than the very best new hires.

In professional firms, it is possible to earn substantially more using high quality personnel, over the long-term, than is possible using lesser quality personnel. The reason for this is that partner income is a function of the profit contribution of the people underlying the partner group. The higher those persons' compensation and abilities are, the higher will be the per employee contribution to the firm's gross profit. By going for the very best quality individual who can learn more, do more, and progress faster, a professional organization will maximize its profit contribution. This conclusion is based on the prevailing practice of relating billing rates to compensation. Clients will not mind, for example, paying $65 an hour for a senior associate who is really able, even though he may have arrived at senior status a year or two before that of a lesser individual who would command only a $48 per hour billing rate. Obviously, if a normal one-third profit contribution factor is enjoyed by the firm, the higher billing rates of the better quality people will produce a higher gross profit contribution per capita. Since operating expenses vary according to headcount, the lesser number of higher value people will produce a higher contribution for a given level of billings.

Another way of expressing this concept is to say that it will be more profitable, relatively speaking, to employ a lesser number of really good people than it will be to muddle along with average people, even though the average folks may cost less and bill for less in the short run.

It took several years to change the hiring practices of the firm described above but the results were impressive. Over approximately a four-year period that organization's profit available for distribution to the partners increased from 13% of revenue to approximately 22% of revenue. And, more importantly, based on the trend, the firm was in a position to improve its performance even further once the system had begun to work.

Quality recruiting cannot be done without an adequate plan. Every professional organization should prepare at least annually a hiring plan covering several future years as a part of their normal business planning exercise. The hiring plan should contemplate the firm's expected growth and work hour requirements and should provide for enough people, considering dropouts and terminations, to maintain an adequate work force based upon forecasted volumes. (See Chapter 15 for more on this.) Remember, it is always possible (although not necessarily desirable) to eliminate excess personnel, but it is very difficult to obtain needed quality people on short notice in a professional environment.

In my professional management experience, I have found it never to be necessary to terminate people arbitrarily because of the fall-off in hours where actual business volume did not reach forecast. This is an important management concept to repeat. The use of the PROFESSIONAL EXCELLENCE system in motivating and managing professional people permits the identification of those whose goals do not coincide with the goals and needs of the firm, early enough so that there is usually plenty of time to allow such people to leave the firm with their heads held high, going to new positions where their personal goals can better be met. Adjusting headcount in the firm, therefore, becomes a matter of accelerating or decelerating the inevitable.

The morale consequences of letting people resign at strategic points to seek their own best directions is very positive as to the rest of the organization. When people feel good about it and know that they, too, will be treated fairly and will not be "defrocked" in front of their peers. Also, this type of treatment will permit a sales force of loyal firm alumni to be built in your community over a number of years. The value of that sales force cannot be underestimated.

In actual practice, your recruiting strategy should contemplate always seeking the very best people available. Even though the number of individuals coming to the market from professional schools has increased markedly in recent years, the top ten percent of the graduating class is still the most desirable group to employ. The better firms will always be competing for that top ten percent and the task of getting good employees is not becoming any easier. In both accounting and law, for example, the number of available graduates has increased threefold since the early seventies. The number of really qualified graduates has scarcely increased by a few percentage points! As indicated in the example above, good people should cost more. More importantly, they can be billed for more. The vibrant energy, trainability and overall excellence of the top ten percent of the class makes the "average" graduate pale in comparison where the professional firm's needs are involved.

One step that I have consistently used in helping to identify these good people is to cultivate sources that will help identify "comers" before the competition does. One way of doing this is to cultivate favor among professors, placement people and the like. A professor who is a leader in your profession has a vested interest in placing his best graduates in the best firms. His success is mirrored by their success. Thus, if you can convince a selected group of educators that your firm is really out for the best people and will go to some lengths to obtain them, you may have the opportunity of being "tipped off" to those people long before the regular recruiting season begins.

Some years ago I got a call from the Chairman of the Accounting Department of the University of Rhode Island. He indicated that one of his best students had obtained his education almost entirely through scholarship assistance but was having some difficulty in his senior year and needed a part-time job. The Chairman went on to say that he was almost positive that the firm which gave the student some part-time work during his senior year would have a prime opportunity to employ him after graduation. It turned out that this young person was truly outstanding and while we had thought the part-time job would merely be a gift we obtained more benefit than we had ever expected. Since the individual had learned to live with and was comfortable with our people as a result of his part-time work, there was only one choice when it came time for graduation. He became a partner of the firm in a very short period of time.

Placement officers, on the other hand, do not usually have the inside track to the leading students, although they should not be ignored. They are extremely helpful in institutions where cooperative study programs are in effect. Under the typical co-op program students take one or two semesters in their junior and senior years to work in the profession of their chosing. The school will typically set a rate of pay based upon market conditions and assign the students to the firms indicating a desire for co-op hires. Even though you typically do not have a choice as to who is assigned to your office, having the favor of the placement director will help you obtain the better quality students. Again, once they have the opportunity of working with you and your people, the decision at graduation is usually almost automatic. And, you have the luxury of not making an offer to a co-op student if it turns out that his trial period with you was not satisfactory.

The above experience with the young man having financial difficulties in his senior year also exemplified the concept of making strategic long-range investments in people before they are hirable. Every now and then, if your community contacts are reasonably good, you will hear about the offspring of some important community leader or a deserving minority student who is looking for some guidance in selection of a career. Several hours invested in interviewing such an individual can pay off in spades some years later. It is always wise to be brutally frank about such a person's potential for advancement in your profession. For example, it is not unusual to have a leading banker call you and say that his son would like to be, say, an architect. You may find the young individual has had a high school grade record that is below average. Then is the appropriate time to express firmly the requirement that the youngster's grades in college must be A's and B's, or else. The parent will appreciate it and if the young person succeeds, he, too, will appreciate your advice.

Strategic long-range investments in people take many forms, some of which are monetary and some of which are simply advisory in nature. Their cost is so insubtantial in comparison with the potential benefit, they should be a firm part of your strategic hiring plan. Hopefully, such investments will be adopted by all of your partners and collegues, (subject to your review as the chief executive) in furthering your organization's hiring objectives.

Another feature in the PROFESSIONAL EXCELLENCE system of professional management involves using all levels of personnel in the recruiting process. For example, in campus recruiting, students are impressed by meeting the individual who has been with your firm, say, a year or two. The recruit can hear actual experiences and gain an understanding of the early development process. Your young people can do more than will be the case where campus recruiting is done entirely by middle level or higher level personnel. That is not to say that campus visits should be made only by juniors. The managing partner or other senior management personnel should be visible on campus and should be involved in the screening in appropriate ways.

Typically, however, when a professional firm goes to a campus for recruiting visits, students are allowed to sign up, randomly at will, for interviews. The interview on campus is a mutual screening process. You will do better in attracting good people to your office for final interviews if you use people who have an empathy with the views of the potential recruits (i.e. your juniors and semi-seniors). But, certain precautions are required.

Never bring someone into your office for a series of final interviews if, in the combined judgment of those involved in the campus recruiting process, you do not think the individual is capable of receiving a final offer. The tendency on the part of some younger people when first exposed to the campus recruiting process is to leave the hard judgments to the people back at the office. This can be fatal. Excessive office interviews cost a great deal of money and will produce a negative image on campus far worse than if rejections are made quickly and cleanly on the basis of campus interviews.

When selected recruits are brought into the office for final evaluation, their evaluation should be extensive and as complex as is needed to assure that a good judgment will be made. The primary objective of the office interview process is to sell the recruit on coming with your firm. Nonetheless, successive interviews with persons at different levels of the organization will enable soft spots or previously unidentified deficiencies to be ascertained. The "selling" of the recruit is based upon exposing him to all levels of the organization over a sufficient period of time that he feels comfortable with those with whom he is ultimately going to work. Stress interviews are not necessary if the office interview is long enough so that a number of in-depth evaluations can be obtained. As a consequence, recruits will not be "turned off" by undue pressure during the office interview process.

On the other hand, good recruiting involves the selective recruiting of experienced people as well. Here, stress interviews can be quite useful in evaluating whether a potential experienced hire has the necessary "stuff" to fit well in your organization. If you are not comfortable in conducting a stress interview yourself, I suggest you obtain some training. You can do this by getting individual counseling from an industrial psychologist at a local university, or participating in some of the courses that are offered for this purpose. One technique I have used with success in the past is the assessment center technique. Here, you assemble a group of assessors who put several recruits through a sample task (such as a proposal presentation). The assessors grade the interviewees on the basis of their relative performance under the stress of a simulated "real life" situation.

The selective use of experienced people can help buttress your organization by enabling you to fill holes that are unexpected. Occasionally, despite well laid plans, an individual who has high promise decides to leave your organization. You need to maintain a balance in the pyramid structure. Further, supervision of important jobs may suffer if you do not have such a pyramid and adequate supervision of your younger people. While the use of experienced hires involves taking a greater degree of risk than relying entirely on people developed and built-up through your own organization, sometimes such risks are reasonable and pay off in the long run. In one situation in which I was involved, a large computer manufacturer had hiring practices that developed a fairly significant number of "cast-offs." These people, on closer inspection, turned out not to be unworthy individuals. The fact was that the manufacturer's employee development system was defective. Accordingly, they would hire significant numbers of bright young people in their systems groups, give them a reasonable amount of initial training and turn them loose for a period of several years. Since the manufacturer had no systematic development process to enable these energetic and able young people to climb the ladder within the organization, they soon became dissatisfied and commenced looking elsewhere. We picked up a number of well qualified systems people every year by passing the word to the manufacturer's organization through their alumni in our employ that our organization was a good place to work. The success of this process developed a continuing stream of well qualified people.

In another circumstance, an organization with which I was working had the opportunity to hire several persons passed over for partnership in competing firms. Careful inquiry and evaluation disclosed that these individuals had been passed over for reasons which were not substantial. In one case, politics had apparently reared its ugly head and the individual had been "backed by" the wrong partners. In another case, the partners had concluded that they could not admit any more partners to the firm. Neither of these reasons were enough to dissuade our evaluators that the individuals would not continue their progress in the profession and make good partners over the long haul. Naturally, a year or two of working in the new firm was necessary before the individual could be finally promoted. However, in both cases the potential partners realized they had to take a step backward for a period of time and felt the investment was worthwhile. In many large professional firms, there is an implied "stamp of approval" that occurs with people who are developed entirely within the organization. It is, in those cases, very difficult to overcome the presumption that anyone from another firm is unqualified. The managing and senior partners must take a great deal of pride in their organization and must convey a sense of espirit de corps but these characteristics should not prohibit the selective recruiting of experienced people.

Balancing the pyramid of the organization is very important. Recruiting of new hires and experienced people is the only way this balancing can be maintained. A useful technique in maintaining the balance is to prepare a five-year promotion forecast every year. One organization I know now requires the managing partner of its practice units to prepare promotion forecasts for all personnel above the middle level as a result of my recommendation. This enables the top management of the firm to identify several years in advance the potential numbers in its management group. Since the management group has several levels, the promotion forecast enables an evaluation of the size and shape of the pyramid which can be compared with the size and shape of the business. Until I originated the promotion forecast in a formal sense, the firm had merely relied upon estimates that were conveyed during annual reviews of the offices. These estimates turned out to be wildly inaccurate on occasion and led to significant distortions in the number of partners admitted in some years. While such distortions can be lived with, another aspect of the promotion forecast is that it forces early identifiction of possible terminations. By avoiding surprises, and forcing an assessment of those who may leave the firm in future periods, you and your firm can do a much better job in maintaining the balance and shape of your pyramid than you would otherwise.

The balance and shape of your pyramid is a key determinent of your organization's profitablity. As noted in the examples above, shooting low in hiring quality can only hurt you in the long run. But simply hiring good people is not enough. The ten "how-to" steps employed in strategic hiring practices with PROFES-SIONAL EXCELLENCE will help you improve and maintain your profitability over the long run. The final segment of the PROFESSIONAL EXCELLENCE system is obvious — it is the business plan.

EXHIBIT 18
How to USE
STRATEGIC HIRING PRACTICES
with PROFESSIONAL EXCELLENCE

1. Prepare and use a hiring plan covering several years, as a part of your business plan.

2. Always seek the best people.

3. Cultivate sources to identify the "comers" before your competition does.

4. Make some strategic long-range investments in people long before they are hireable.

5. Never decline a special interview if requested by a business/community contact.

6. Be frank and fair early on.

7. Use all levels in the recruiting process.

8. Selectively recruit experienced people.

9. Balance your pyramids.

10. Every year prepare a 5-year promotion forecast.

CHAPTER 15

HAVE A RATIONAL BUSINESS PLAN

"If you don't know where you're going,
you will go somewhere else."
— Lawrence J. Peter

Making a professional service organization into a vibrant and dynamic entity is not without risk. But the risk is not in the technology of the service itself, it is in the care and skill with which the management of the organization is conducted. The systems involved in personnel management and motivation in PROFES-SIONAL EXCELLENCE are fairly straight forward, even if unusual, as the preceding chapters of this book have demonstrated. However, even though it is easy to know where you want to go, there will be many variations in strategy and technique needed to adapt the operating realities of each particular organization. Many manufacturing, distribution and retail execu-tives are astonished to learn that quite a number of their professional advisors do not have formal written business plans. Yet, it is just as important to do capacity planning and make strategic investment decisions in professional firms as it is in a manufacturing business.

Implementing a systematic approach to managing a professional practice or service organization is easy.

The concepts are readily grasped and most of them are accepted in the main by the typically intelligent and rational people that populate the professions. Planning for growth and effectiveness involves targeting opportunities while operating systems are being implemented. Concentrating on technical strengths and your competitor's weaknesses won't happen by accident.

For example, one strategy that I have used for many years is to selectively offer services that competing professional firms did not. Generally, these services are to be found emerging at the leading edge of managerial technology. Thus, in the case of each such new service, professional capabilities had to be obtained, as opposed to adapting them from existing service systems. One example is the use of personnel services in the CPA firm environment. While many CPA firms have done recruiting and have assisted management in the evaluation of financial personnel, the emerging technologies of EEO (Equal Employment Opportunity) and non-discriminatory methods of employee selection and promotion are brand new technologies. For us to offer such services, seemed entirely normal since they are highly numerical and statistically oriented, yet to be able to provide them we had to train selected partners in such techniques so they could effectively supervise them. We had to go out and employ capable people with necessary underlying education backgrounds. This required an investment. The investment was not possible until it was made a part of our long-range business plan. Then it had to be made a part of each year's business budget. A forecast of revenues and profit contribution from the new service was an integral part of the planning for the investment. Entering into such service did not happen by accident, and making the investment required an effort.

Criteria for investing in such "leading edge" services included the following guidelines:

a. An economic future for the service could be identified (i.e. profitable and growing fee volume).
b. The work could be effectively supervised by a member of the firm (i.e. it is understood, wanted and supervised by a partner level person).
c. People to provide the service were obtainable (i.e. adequate training, reasonable supply).
d. Quality work could be done (i.e. quality and assurance was both possible and economic).

The use of "leading edge" technology as a development tool for the professional service organization is but one of the many strategies that should be contemplated in setting the course for the firm's future.

Is there an ideal approach for business planning in a professional service organization? Obviously not, but a rational business plan needs at least the same elements of profit planning, resource consideration, turnover calculation, market evaluation, strategic elements, recruiting and so forth that a business plan requires for a non-service organization. More often than not, the biggest change in managing through the use of a business plan in a professional firm is in communication and in bringing the business plan out into the open, putting it into writing and exposing to the rest of the organization.

Even if a professional firm does not have a rational written business plan, it has a business plan. The consequences of not identifying where you want to concentrate your efforts, for example, are just as important as the rational decisions involved in picking those areas you wish to emphasize. As stated above, turning a professional service organization into a highly profitable, vibrant and dynamic entity is not without risk. But the risk is not in the technology of management, for the systems are straight forward and easily implemented. Thus, it is very important to know where you want to go and how to get there although there will be variations in technique to adapt to the realities of each particular firm.

If there are risks and problems they will usually surface in timing and in communication. Some people can take more change than others. Thus, it is vitally important to have adequate participation in developing your firm's business plan. Without adequate participation your people may not accept any change at all. Discerning the needs of the individuals in your organization can take long periods of time, and communicating such needs to others in the group will usually take a multiple of the time involved in opening the organization to exploration of such real needs. The seven how to steps involved in the PROFESSIONAL EXCELLENCE business plan are simple. In setting them forth in Exhibit 19, they have been put in what is actually the reverse order of their development. In fact, the development process is usually an interactive one in which the first step listed in Exhibit 19 results from a series of successive approximations initially arrived at in steps 4 and 5 of the "how-to" list. They are listed in conceptual order in Exhibit 19, rather than implementation sequence, to help you visualize and organize how the business plan in conceived.

In any organization, however, it's difficult to start with the very broad and general without having a relatively firm grounding in the present and specific. Thus, I recommend that you start your rational business plan with an annual short-term business budget. This will tell you what is immediately do-able and achievable. By building personnel, training, practice development and other aspects of your plan into the short-term budget you will see "how much will fit." Adjustments in both the short-term and longer range budgets are inevitable. Meanwhile, as the short-term plan is being prepared, the partners (in particular) and management group of your organization should look at your strengths and weaknesses and decide how they wish to concentrate their efforts for building the firm in the directions they desire. Some of the strategies that I have described in earlier chapters are samples of how professional firms have concentrated on their strengths and overcome their weaknesses, or taken advantage of competitors' weaknesses.

A formal systems planning approach to developing your strategies would include the following step-by-step factors:

1. Analyze your own internal situation: strengths, weaknesses, competencies, problems.

2. Project current services, profits, revenues, investment needs into the future.

3. Analyze selected external environment factors and your competitor's potential, actions, and opportunities.

4. Establish broad goals as targets for subordinate group plans.

5. Identify the gap between expected and desired results, if such a gap exists.

6. Communicate planning assumptions to your operating divisions.*

---

* In a CPA Firm these might be audit department, tax department and management consulting; in a law firm they might be litigation department, corporate department, tax department, securities department and trusts and estates.

7. Request preliminarly operating plans from the divisions with specific target goals, resource needs and supporting action plans identified.

8. Request special studies of alternatives, contingencies and longer-term opportunities as such occasions arise.

9. Review and improve divisional plans and combine them for the overall organization picture.

10. Develop long-term budgets related to such plans.

11. Revise short and long-term budgets based upon needed adjustments in resource allocation, operating results and the like.

12. Publish final plans and budgets and communicate with appropriate ceremony and dignity.

13. Assign specific responsibility for implementing both normal operating and special strategic elements of the budgets and plans.

14. Monitor and evaluate performance comparing with plans and budgets on no less than a monthly basis.

This approach tends to focus heavily on measurable quantitative factors and may, if not compensated for, underemphasize the qualitative organizational and power/behaviorial factors which often determine strategic success in one situation versus another. In practice, such planning is just a building block in the continuous stream of events that really determine a business' strategy. In reviewing studies of business planning over the years, I have identified some factors that should be considered in developing your rational business plan. Among other things, consider the following:

— Organizations usually have multiple goal structures; recognize them.

— Strategic decisions are not immune to political factors; be sensitive.

— Coalitions may affect strategic management; create the right ones.

— Executive bargaining and negotiating is part of the process; let it occur naturally.

— Satisfying (as opposed to maximizing) is typical in professional organizations; don't try to be perfect.

— When satisfactory decisions cannot be made intellectually, the practice of "muddling along" sometimes results.

"Muddling along" is reality. While some sophisticates have popularized MBWA (managing by wandering around), muddling is a more realistic management tool. A series of successful approximations is usually better than a perfect initial solution.

Ways of dealing with these factors include making sure that strategies emerge from a series of a strategic sub-systems each of which attacks a specific issue or a specific class of issues. These can be addressed in a disciplined way much more easily if they are approached in small steps. A cohesive firm strategy can emerge from the pyramid of such small decisions.

When sub-systems and divisional plans are developed, the logic behind them usually become sufficiently powerful that they serve as a normative basis for the organization's overall plan. In other words, even though it may look like "muddling", developing a business plan in small logical increments is often a useful technique and can form a successful basis for combining the hard data aspects of a business plan with the social and political aspects.

Another example of strategically incremental decisions is involved in the assessment of competitors' and the market's weaknesses. By identifying strategic opportunities in advance but not necessarily exploiting them all at once, communication and action time lines can be compressed when it is appropriate for such opportunities to be taken advantage of. In other words, when the organization is ready for taking a planned major step, but for budget or other reasons has not yet taken it, it is much easier to implement the change or strategy than it would be if it was new at the time when implementation was proposed.

Building a comfort factor in risk taking is another way of overcoming resistance to change in developing a business plan. Peoples' perceptions of risk are enhanced when they are not knowledgeable about a particular field. A well conceived diversification program or strategic plan should acknowledge that a trial and error period during which top managers reject early propositions is normal. "Trial balloons" if floated often enough may help to overcome perceived risk. And, a sure way of overcoming perceived risk is to make sure that there are enough early successes in changing the direction of the organization's thrust so that later strategies have a better acceptance rate.

The willingness to strategically phase-out certain services or certain groups of personnel surely requires a great deal of managerial courage. Again, doing it on a strategically opportunistic basis with small experimental moves before attempting large and significant ones is a way of enhancing success when the important moves come along.

Appendix 4 shows a ten-year income projection for a typical professional firm having an opening head-count of about 100 people. This document is an example of the typical form in which the long-range business plan would be summarized in hard data. Some of the typical strategic planning assumptions are implicit in the information derived from the income statement presented in the projection. Examples are the number of people at various levels and the changes in those levels over the priod of time. If a firm plans in business segment divisions, as suggested above, there should obviously be divisional projections underlying this summary. There may also be an administrative or overhead section. Detailed profiles of each expense line should be prepared by each division in preparing the projection, however, the profile detail need only be prepared for the first few years unless a significant change in expense characteristics is expected (such as an out of proportion change in insurance expense, for example). You will also note that the ten-year projection is expressed in terms of constant dollars, as exemplified by the average amount of billing per staff member. It is much easier to do projections of this sort in constant dollars then to assume inflation rates. When inflationary changes occur they will tend to occur at all levels. It is important, however, to match billing rates to changes in salary levels and to be alert to distortions well enough in advance not to be caught "behind the power curve." At least the first year's budget should be developed in much greater detail than the summary projections. Among other things, gross income should be projected on the basis of pricing out estimated work levels for known clients with a factor added for projected client additions and losses. To that should be added the effect of an evaluation of historical changes in income patterns. For example, if litigation support has historically had a 25% per year growth, whereas trust and estates is only growing at the rate of 3% per year, those factors should be considered in addition to pricing out specific client's work.

Now look at Appendix 5 for an example of a five-year staffing plan. The Exhibit is derived from a very good article prepared by James F. Rabenhorst, that appeared in the Autumn 1979 issue of "Today's Executive" published by Price Waterhouse & Co., New York.* It shows in steps how a typical professional firm might develop a staffing plan to maintain the validity of its pyramids and provide for future growth. The assumptions made by the preparers of the plan are given in steps 2 and 7. The steps were basically to identify the present staffing situation of the firm, develop some planning assumptions, prepare a preliminary five-year plan, compare the preliminary plan with some actual information for the first few years and then determine the results of the firm's ability to implement its objectives. This, then, leads to identifying problems, preparing some planning alternatives and to new assumptions. The preparation of a substantially revised five-year plan can then take place. As the revised plan has begun to be implemented, results can be compared in the early years and the process can begin again. It is also useful to compare the first planning effort with the revised effort to see where the major changes have occurred and to evaluate the results. Step 11 shows some interesting ratios of partners to associates in the firm. Obviously, the firm in this example needed to step up its recruiting rather substantially.

Many professionals will ask themselves what role

---

* reproduced with permission.

classical formal planning techniques should play in formulating their own business strategy. Almost all firms have some type of planning, the degree of formality of which varies according to the interests and abilities of management. Formal planning procedures serve a number of essential functions and I believe the more formal your planning efforts the better your results will be. Planning with hard data and making tough decisions will:

— Provide discipline to force managers to look ahead periodically.

— Require rigorous communication about goals, issues and resource allocations.

— Stimulate longer-term analyses than would have otherwise been made.

— Generate a basis for evaluating and integrating short-term plans.

— Lengthen time horizons and protect long-term investments.

— Create a backdrop and information network about the future, against which the leaders of the firm can calibrate results and interim decisions.

In other words, using formal planning techniques enables you to fine tool your annual commitments, formalize strategic programs and help implement changes that are needed once they are decided upon by your management group.

In a professional firm, it is almost impossible to assign the planning process to an individual or group of individuals who are separate from the day-to-day management of the firm. In order to utilize the expertise and obtain the commitment of the people in your organization planning should occur from the bottom up — this means broad participation and lengthy preparation. Of course, lower level groups will have only a partial view of your overall strategy and will command only a fragment of the resources available to top management. Also, the power base and identity of people lower in the organization depends upon, to a much greater extent than top management, the existing services the firm is rendering. Thus, there is a tendency for existing services to receive most of the attention of people lower in the organization. You will have to provide most of the thrust in new directions as a result. A useful approach in designing your rational business plan is to make sure it is a "living thing." Use it as a framework to guide and provide consistency for future decisions and to force strategic assessments today rather than tomorrow.

Having a rational business plan will pull together the management techniques involved in PROFESSIONAL EXCELLENCE. This system will enable you to earn more because your earnings will be what you have planned them to be to a much greater extent than if the various personnel motivation and management techniques described in this book are not employed. Some of the techniques I have described are considered to be unusual, even to the extent of being considered "far-out" by some professional people. But, they work and they have demonstrated their validity in many successful professional organizations.

EXHIBIT 19
How to have a
RATIONAL BUSINESS PLAN
using PROFESSIONAL EXCELLENCE

1. Always prepare a written annual (short-term) business budget.

2. Build personnel, training, practice development plans into the short-term budget.

3. Build long-range strategies and investments into the short-term budget.

4. Develop such long-range strategies and investments by first having a five-year (or longer) forecast and plan.

5. Plan for future directions and identify strengths and weakness that need to be addressed to have a balanced plan.

6. Use participative techniques to assure that all levels have appropriate input into the plan.

7. Always summarize plan directions, conclusions and alternatives in writing.

Also see — description of formal systems planning steps described in Chapter 15.

POSTSCRIPT

There you have it!

The use of the system described in this book is a proven and demonstrated technique. I have used it for many years, and have helped numerous others apply this system. My use, of course, has been evolving over the 14 years I was a managing partner of several large offices of a CPA firm and later in consulting to various other professional organizations. As the integration of the techniques became better understood and more and more standardized, the system's benefits improved commensurably. None of the techniques are revolutionary although some of them may be regarded by some professionals as further than their experience would have led them to conclude one could go in managing bright, aggressive and intelligent people. It is the fact that you want your professional people to be bright, aggressive and intelligent that makes it necessary to use techniques which go further than the traditional. The key to the system is, however, its complete integration and the reliance in one part of the system upon building blocks that have been developed in other parts. It is possible that improvements could be made in your operation by applying only some of the system, but I can assure you that the full potential will not be achieved if you do not take advantageof the entire integrated whole. PROFESSIONAL EXCELLENCE is a system.

You will undoubtably find that variations will occur in how to apply the system. You may apply it differently at first than you will once you have become comfortable in using it on a day-to-day basis. Also, your firm's needs and conditions will change as your business evolves using the system. If you would like assistance or wish

to discuss any aspect of PROFESSIONAL EXCEL-
LENCE as applies to your firm do not hesitate to contact me and I will provide as much help as I possibly
can.

Although the profitability of your practice is not
necessarily assured, only you can do that, it certainly
will be enhanced through application of the system. To
that end I wish you success in using PROFESSIONAL
EXCELLENCE and satisfaction in bringing home the
results!

APPENDIX I

CAREER CAPABILITY PROFILE
(Typical CPA Firm Environment)

1. An <u>entry-level</u> senior should be able to:
   a. Start building personal contacts for the future
   b. Identify new work situations in regular clients
   c. Manage completely, through report or return preparation one client at a time
   d. Start engaging in civic and voluntary interests
   e. Train, train, train

2. A <u>senior</u> should be able to:
   a. Do all of the above
   b. Identify add-ons and new work situations in each client for which he is responsible
   c. Assist manager in developing b. items into engagements
   d. Build personal contacts into work possibilities
   e. Participate effectively in technical activities (State society, professional groups)
   f. Demonstrate beginning of career path to "control positions" in civic and voluntary interests
   g. Manage up to 5 or 6 <u>jobs</u> at one time, depending upon complexity
   h. Train, train, train

3. A <u>manager</u> should be able to:
   a. Do all of the above
   b. Sell add-ons and new work situations
   c. Upgrade personal and business contacts into new work opportunities
   d. Branch out into social organizations
   e. Obtain leadership roles (control) in civic, social and voluntary interests

f. Demonstrate unchallenged technical competence
g. Write and speak without any problems
h. Manage on complete responsibility basis (front-line) multiple clients
i. Train, train, train

4. A principal should be able to:
   a. Do all of the above
   b. Identify new business, size-up, seize opportunities and convert into clients
   c. Effectively transfer technical responsibilities to manager and senior levels
   d. Act as partner on several smaller clients at once or up to 3 large clients
   e. Communicate completely, "hands' down" writing and speaking ability
   f. Consistently demonstrate superior judgment
   g. Expand relationships to bring other persons in the firm into his contact areas
   h. Train, train, train

5. A partner should be able to:
   a. Do all of the above
   b. Provide strategic sense and direction
   c. Exercise faultless judgment
   d. Prospect, cold or hot, and sell easily
   e. Plan, lead and look ahead
   f. Train, train, train

APPENDIX 2

SALARY MODEL
Promotion frequency — annual

LEVEL	Unsatisfactory T	Adequate 3-0%	Satisfactory 0-6%	Above Average 6-10%	Outstanding 10-15%
New hire	—	—	14-16,000	—	—
Semi-senior	—	450-0	0-900 14,900-16,900	900-1500	1500-2250
Senior	—	500-0	0-1000 15,900-16,900	1000-1600	1600-2400
Manager	—	510-0	0-1100 16,500-17,500	1100-1700	1700-2500
Principal	—				
Partner	—				

T = terminate

Note — Figures are illustrative only — in actual practice wider differentiation between levels may be desirable. The above scale assumes three years to manager level. A typical growth will be salary doubling by manager level if a six-year period is required for moving through the ranks. Another 30% will be then required for principal if it takes three-four years.

APPENDIX 3

COMPANY ENGAGEMENT
PERFORMANCE REVIEW

Name _____ Title _____ Date _____

Period covered _____ Report prepared by _____

Client engagements during period   Specific tasks performed   INSTRUCTIONS: Circle appropriate number, and enter brief comments to support the rating. See rating explanation below.

_____   _____

_____   _____

_____   _____

_____   _____

_____
(Reviewer's signature)

A.   DETAIL APPRAISAL   RATING

1. Knowledge and Skills Know and use basic fundamentals, techniques, and procedures? His field of strength? Others? Self-development effort? Adequate inter-relating of skills?		1	2	3	4	5
2. Analytical Ability Properly and thoroughly "think through" problems, secure proper facts, evaluate and reach sound conclusions?		1	2	3	4	5
3. Quality of Work Work meet standard requirements? Professional level? Practical and acceptable ideas and recommendations? Work through and complete? Follow through? Creative?		1	2	3	4	5
4. Quantity of Work Accomplish objectives on time? Extra effort? Willing to work beyond normal hours?		1	2	3	4	5
5. Planning and organizing Plan ahead, schedule, lay out work to effectively use own time and others? Drive?		1	2	3	4	5
6. Self Expression Use of good English? Vocabulary range? Minimum of jargon? Clear concise written reports?	Oral: Written:	1 1	2 2	3 3	4 4	5 5
7. Personality Effect on others (Firm personnel and/or client personnel), disposition, tact, manner, enthusiasm, bearing, appearance, etc.?		1	2	3	4	5
8. Attitude Positive? Inquiring? Progressive? Empathy for other opinions? Acceptance of guidance and instruction?		1	2	3	4	5

9. Judgment — Maturity	1	2	3	4	5

9. Judgment — Maturity
Mature thinker, talker and performer? Stability under
pressure? Able to evaluate what is more or less
important? Long term point of view?

10. Leadership Qualities	1	2	3	4	5

10. Leadership Qualities
Inspire respect and confidence in firm and/or
client personnel? Show initiative and drive? Clear
instructions? Decisiveness? Persuasiveness?
Impact on clients?

*EXPLANATION OF RATINGS: (1) Fails to meet job requirements; (2) Meets minimum job requirements; (3) Meets job
requirements; (4) Clearly exceeds job requirements; (5) Rarely equalled in exceeding job requirements.*

B.   SUMMARY APPRAISAL

1. Over-all   1   2   3   4   5

2. Strengths

3. Weaknesses

4. Recommendations (including training)

C.   REVIEW WITH INDIVIDUAL   (Date discussed with individual:)

1. Reaction to Discussion

2. Individual Goals

3. Follow Up

APPENDIX 4

Ten-year Income Projection
in Thousands of Dollars

	Budget 1979/80	1980/81	1981/82	1982/83	1983/84	1984/85	1985/86	1986/87	1987/88	1988/89
Gross income	$ 5,614	$ 6,631	$ 7,975	$ 9,346	$11,098	$12,938	$15,429	$17,918	$20,956	$24,449
Expenses										
Payroll										
Professional staff	$ 1,659	$ 2,052	$ 2,754	$ 3,474	$ 4,199	$ 4,911	$ 5,880	$ 6,853	$ 8,043	$ 9,414
	(29.55%)	(30.94%)	(34.53%)	(37.17%)	(37.84%)	(37.95%)	(38.11%)	(38.24%)	(38.38%)	(38.50%)
Paraprofessional staff	125	148	171	187	203	221	241	254	770	284
	(2.23%)	(2.23%)	(2.15%)	(2.00%)	(1.83%)	(1.71%)	(1.56%)	(1.42%)	(1.29%)	(1.16%)
Administrative staff	371	431	478	514	555	647	771	896	1,048	1,222
	(6.61%)	(6.50%)	(6.00%)	(5.50%)	(5.00%)	(5.00%)	(5.00%)	(5.00%)	(5.00%)	(5.00%)
Other expenses	1,693	1,790	1,914	2,056	2,442	2,846	3,394	3,942	4,610	5,379
	(30.16%)	(27.00%)	(24.00%)	(22.00%)	(22.00%)	(22.00%)	(22.00%)	(22.00%)	(22.00%)	(22.00%)
Total	$ 3,848	$ 4,421	$ 5,317	$ 6,231	$ 7,399	$ 8,625	$10,286	$11,945	$13,971	$16,299
	(31.45%)	(33.00%)	(33.00%)	(33.00%)	(33.00%)	(33.00%)	(33.00%)	(33.00%)	(33.00%)	(33.00%)
Net income	$ 1,766	$ 2,210	$ 2,658	$ 3,115	$ 3,699	$ 4,313	$ 5,143	$ 5,973	$ 6,985	$ 8,150
	(31.45%)	(33.00%)	(33.00%)	(33.00%)	(33.00%)	(33.00%)	(33.00%)	(33.00%)	(33.00%)	(33.00%)
No. partners/principals	26	28	33	39	44	49	56	60	66	75
No. professional staff	73	90	110	130	156	183	220	257	303	355
No. paraprofessional staff	9	11	12	13	14	15	16	17	18	19
Average net income per partner/principal	$67,900	$78,900	$80,500	$79,900	$84,100	$88,000	$91,800	$99,600	$105,800	$108,700
Average income of professional staff	$22,700	$22,800	$25,000	$26,700	$26,900	$26,800	$26,700	$26,700	$26,500	$26,500
Average income of paraprofessional staff	$13,900	$13,500	$14,400	$14,500	$14,700	$15,000	$15,000	$15,000	$15,000	$15,000

Computation of Partners and Principals

	1979/80	1980/81	1981/82	1982/83	1983/84	1984/85	1985/86	1986/87	1987/88	1988/89
Number of partners/principals—September 30	23	26	28	33	39	44	49	56	60	66
Partner changes at October 1										
Merged partners	0	1	2	1	2	1	2	1	2	2
Retired partners	0	0	0	0	0	0	0	(1)	(1)	(1)
New partners	2	1	3	4	3	4	3	4	5	8
New principals	1	0	0	1	0	0	2	0	0	0
Total at end of year	26	28	33	39	44	49	56	60	66	75
Gross billing per partner/principal	$215,900	$236,800	$241,700	$239,600	$252,200	$264,000	$275,500	$298,600	$317,500	$326,000

Computation of Number of Professional Staff Based on Income in Thousands of Dollars

	Budget 1979/80	1980/81	1981/82	1982/83	1983/84	1984/85	1985/86	1986/87	1987/88	1988/89
Estimated income	$ 5,614	$ 6,631	$ 7,975	$ 9,346	$11,098	$12,938	$15,429	$17,918	$20,956	$24,449
Less partners'/principals' portion (1)	1,572	1,857	2,233	2,617	3,107	3,623	4,320	5,017	5,868	6,846
Balance to determine staff requirements	$ 4,042	$ 4,774	$ 5,742	$ 6,729	$ 7,991	$ 9,315	$11,109	$12,901	$15,088	$17,603
Divided by average amount of billing per staff member (2)	$47,000	$47,000	$47,000	$47,000	$47,000	$47,000	$47,000	$47,000	$47,000	$47,000
Number of staff	86	101	122	143	170	198	236	274	321	374

(For the purpose of finding the average income of the professional staff in our ten-year plan, the average of these two computations is used.)

(1) For the purpose of this computation, the firm-wide 1978/79 ratio was used which is 28%.

(2) As the firm expands, this amount may change;

(2) As the firm expands, this amount may change; however, for the purpose of determining how many people to hire, $47,000 is used. This is based on the amount of fiscal year 1978/79 fees generated by total professional staff, including paraprofessionals and excluding partners/principals.

From an article "The Art and Science of Picking Your Niche for Growth", by D. P. Zume, March 1980 Practising CPA, Copyright AICPA, Inc., reproduced with permission.

A Look at May, Zima & Co. in 1989

May, Zima & Co. is a firm of 20 offices located throughout the southeastern United States in major metropolitan areas. Total volume is in excess of $24,000,000, and is derived, for the most part, from services rendered to small- and medium-sized organizations. The firm has handled a number of SEC registrations, and performs audits and accounting services for reporting companies and all types of entities in the health care field. The backbone of the practice is the broad-based services to small- and medium-sized organizations with the full range of tax services complementing its audit, accounting and management services capabilities.

The firm is recognized as a leader in the area of not-for-profit organizations with emphasis on governmental agency and service organizations, such as hospitals, and has also developed an early expertise in computer installations.

The total professional staff of approximately 450 people is guided by the firm's 75 partners and principals. The firm's philosophy of close client contact by the owners has resulted in its having a broad group of partners/principals of relatively young average age. The ratio of staff to partners/principals is five to one. The lack of a large-client practice base has discouraged the development of a staff heavily populated with "junior" accountants. The firm has an outstanding reputation on college campuses and is considered to be a young progressive firm which offers quality training and guidance, and challenge coupled with early responsibility and opportunity.

Economic reward has kept pace within the partnership. Average partner/principal income is over $100,000 and the top partners/principals are earning in excess of $150,000. Staff salaries are comparable to those of other large firms, with fringe benefits more favorable for the most part.

The firm has been active professionally both at the state society level and within the structure of the AICPA. Community involvement is the rule of May, Zima & Co., and partners/principals and staff take an active role in all aspects of community life, particularly in the areas of service through clubs, charitable organizations, and local and state governmental organizations.

In summary, May, Zima & Co. in many respects is the same growing, progressive firm that it was 10 years ago — only much larger. The basic firm philosophy has remained intact, and its increased size has enhanced the firm's ability to serve its clients at all levels in a professional, competent manner which combines regional firm professional expertise with local firm client involvement.

Assumptions

The 1979/80 budget was prepared following a conservative philosophy.

The components of the income projections for the years through 1988/89 were computed as follows:

Gross income

To each previous year's gross income, a merger/purchase averaging $175,000 for each partner merged has been added, plus a 15% internal growth factor.

Payroll

☐ *Professional staff*—29.55% of income (based on the 1979/80 budget, including bonuses) increasing to 38.50% in 10 years. National statistics gathered by the AICPA indicate this to be too high; however, it is unlikely this percentage would decrease with the quality of practice and the partner/principal staff ratio we want to maintain.

☐ *Paraprofessional staff*—The employment of nine paraprofessionals with an average annual income of $13,900 is budgeted for fiscal year 1979/80. The number employed will likely increase to 11 in 1980/81, and their average annual income will increase to $15,000 in six years.

☐ *Administrative*—6.61% of income (based on 1979/80 budget) declining to 5% over four years. National statistics gathered by the AICPA indicate this percentage should be 5.2% of income.

Other operating expenses

30.16% of income (based on the 1979/80 budget, excluding partners'/principals' retirement payout). This is too high and will have to be reduced gradually. We must strive to stay within the 1979/80 budget and even cut the percentage if possible. Therefore, for income projections purposes, succeeding fiscal years' other operating expense percentages have been reduced to the following:

1980/81	27%
1981/82	24%
1982/83	22%

It is assumed these expenses will level out to 22% of income in all future years. National statistics gathered by the AICPA indicate this percentage should be 18.3% of income.

Net Income

31.45% of budgeted gross income for 1979/80. The above assumptions of productive payroll leveling out at approximately 40% of volume, nonproductive payroll leveling out at 5% and other operating expenses leveling out at 22% will eventually produce net income of 33%. This seems to be a desirable and attainable level of net income. National statistics indicate it should be 38%. While this percentage would be more desirable, achieving 33% should be our first goal.

Number of partners and principals

As of September 30, 1979, the volume stands at $205,100 per partner and based on the adopted budget for fiscal year 1979/80, will be $215,900 per partner. Based on estimated costs of operating our firm, the volume per partner will need to increase to provide a satisfactory level of average income per partner. This long-range plan is based on the goal of achieving a satisfactory level as soon as possible. Because the level is affected by economic changes, no specific amount is identifiable, but it appears that approximately $300,000 of volume per partner will come close to what we would need under our long-range plan in the present economic conditions. (See computation of Partners and Principals.)

Number of professional staff

Computed as per the attached schedule.

Acquisitions/mergers

Included in this plan is one acquisition/merger a year for the next nine years. For purposes of income projections, each year's acquisition/merger is assumed to take place on October 1.

133

APPENDIX 5

Clark & King
Example of a five-year long-range plan
Staffing

☐ *Step 1*

Clark & King
Present staffing
Partners and Associates

	Year 0
Partner:	
Level III	Clark
Level II	King
Level I	Abbot
	Baker
Associate:	
Level II	Ring
	Smith
Level I	Thomas
	Brown
	Haley

☐ *Step 2*

Clark & King
**Preliminary five-year long-range
plan assumptions**

- Constant dollars used throughout the five-year period
- Average billing rates and billable hours per level remain constant throughout the five-year period
- Hire one associate per year
- After three years of service, an associate is promoted from Level I and Level II associate (there is an attrition rate of one in six—occurring every six years)
- After six years of service, all associates are promoted to partner
- After five years, partners in Level I and Level II progress to next higher level

134

☐ Step 3

Clark & King
Results—preliminary five-year plan

Partner:	Year 0	Year 1	Year 2	Year 3	Year 4	Year 5
Level III	Clark	Clark	Clark	Clark	Clark King	Clark King
Level II	King	King	King	King	Abbot	Abbot Baker
Level I	Abbot Baker	Abbot Baker Ring	Abbot Baker Ring	Abbot Baker Ring Smith	Baker Ring Smith Thomas	Ring Smith Thomas Brown

☐ Step 4

Clark & King
Results—preliminary five-year plan

Associates:	Year 0	Year 1	Year 2	Year 3	Year 4	Year 5
Level II	Ring Smith	Smith Thomas	Smith Thomas Brown	Thomas Brown Haley	Brown Haley Ingram	Haley Ingram
Level I	Thomas Brown Haley	Brown Haley Ingram	Haley Ingram Jones	Ingram Jones Kraft	Jones Kraft Lane	Kraft Lane Monroe

☐ Step 5

Clark & King
Preliminary five-year plan
problem identification

Problem:

Since (year 0 vs. year 5) the number of partners at each level has doubled and the number of associates has remained constant; on a per partner basis the net income contribution by associates has halved.

135

□ Step 6

Clark & King
Preliminary five-year plan
problem identification
and alternatives

Alternatives:

- Accept a reduced per partner net income contribution from the associates
- Change the formula for partner compensation
- Determine other sources of net income
    Increase billing rates and/or billable hours
    Utilize paralegals
- Change associate hiring practices; increase the number of associates to be hired
- Change the promotion policies for associates
    Lengthen the years for associates to be promoted to Level II and to partner
    Increase the attrition rate of associates

□ Step 7

Clark & King
Revised five-year long-range
plan assumptions

- Constant dollars used throughout the five-year period
- Average billing rates and billable hours per level remain constant throughout the five-year period
- Hire two associates per year
- After *four* years of service, an associate is promoted from Level I to Level II associate (there is an attrition rate of one in *four*—occurring at end of year *four*)
- After *eight* years of service, associates are promoted to partner (there is a further attrition, with *one in three terminated* rather than promoted to partner)
- After five years, partners in Level I and Level II progress to the next higher level

136

☐ *Step 8*

Clark & King
Results—Revised five-year plan

	Year 0	Year 1	Year 2	Year 3	Year 4	Year 5
Partner:						
Level III	Clark	Clark	Clark	Clark	Clark King	Clark King
Level II	King	King	King	King	Abbot	Abbot Baker
Level I	Abbot Baker	Abbot Baker Ring	Abbot Baker Ring	Abbot Baker Ring	Baker Ring Thomas	Ring Thomas

☐ *Step 9*

Clark & King
Results—Revised five-year plan

	Year 0	Year 1	Year 2	Year 3	Year 4	Year 5
Associate:						
Level II	Ring Smith	Smith Thomas	Smith Thomas	Thomas Haley	Haley Ingram Ivy	Haley Ingram Ivy Jackson
Level I	Thomas Brown Haley	Brown Haley Ingram Ivy	Haley Ingram Ivy Jones Jackson	Ingram Ivy Jones Jackson Kraft Knight	Jones Jackson Kraft Knight Lane Lynn	Kraft Knight Lane Lynn Monroe Miller

☐ *Step 10*

Clark & King
Results of plans compared

	Year 0	Preliminary plan year 5	Revised plan year 5
Partner:			
Level III	Clark	Clark King	Clark King
Level II	King	Abbot Baker	Abbot Baker
Level I	Abbot Baker	Ring Smith Thomas Brown	Ring Thomas

☐ *Step 11*

Clark & King
Results of plans compared

	Year 0	Preliminary plan year 5	Revised plan year 5
Associate:			
Level III	Ring Smith	Ring Ingram	Haley Ingram Ivy Jackson
Level II	Thomas Brown Haley	Kraft Lane Monroe	Kraft Knight Lane Lynn Monroe Miller
Associate/ Partner ratio	1.2	.62	1.7

This Space Reserved for Personal Notes

This Space Reserved for Personal Notes

This Space Reserved for Personal Notes

This Space Reserved for Personal Notes

This Space Reserved for Personal Notes

This Space Reserved for Personal Notes